PALACE DIARY

The Queen descends the staircase from the royal suite of the Williamsburg Inn, Williamsburg, Virginia, during the royal visit to the United States in 1957. This photograph has been acclaimed as one of the best colour pictures of Her Majesty ever taken. Her American hosts described her gown as of white satin "almost incandescent with embroidery."

"Chicago Tribune," Photo by Al Madsen

Fr.

BRIGADIER STANLEY CLARK O.B.E.

Palace Diary

Authorized account of the crowded days of Queen Elizabeth's life from the time of her twenty-first birthday on April 21, 1947, compiled with full access to her engagement diaries

GEORGE G. HARRAP & CO. LTD

LONDON TORONTO WELLINGTON SYDNEY

First published in Great Britain 1958
by George G. Harrap & Co. Ltd
182 High Holborn, London, W.C.1

© *Brigadier Stanley Clark* 1958

Composed in Bembo type and printed by
Western Printing Services Ltd, Bristol
Made in Great Britain

Preface

THIS book aims at presenting a picture of the daily life of Queen Elizabeth II, Queen of Great Britain and Northern Ireland, Queen of Canada, of Australia, New Zealand, South Africa, Ceylon; Queen of Rhodesia and Nyasaland, of Ghana, of Nigeria, of the West Indies, Malaya, Singapore, Borneo; Queen of Fiji, New Guinea, and of a thousand specks of land which dot the map of the world like stars in the sky; Head of the Commonwealth, and so of India and Pakistan—the acknowledged ruler of more independent territories than any sovereign in history.

Daily, as the development of the Commonwealth of Nations springs powerfully forward, the Queen's responsibilities increase. Daily the pressure on her time becomes greater; the mass of documents coming to her desk becomes more demanding of her energies; the column of aides and advisers requesting audience grows longer; the complexity of her problems is more acute and the difficulty of her decisions more daunting. Yet always when she is at home Her Majesty fulfils her rôle as mistress of the house, deciding details of the domestic work, changes of furniture and furnishings, selecting menus.

Daily, without fail—the only times that her pressing duties will allow—she spends the hour after breakfast and an hour at tea-time with her children. At every week-end when she is in residence at one of the royal homes the

Queen has her children constantly with her, and also usually her mother and sister, for the family ties are very strong. No task stands in the way of the morning attendance at church on Sunday, even if the urgent affairs of State make the rest of the day increasingly like any other.

The Queen chooses all the engagements she carries out. From a list of several thousands each year Her Majesty selects from 400 to 500—always a greater number than her advisers would wish. Into every year the Queen knows she must now fit tours of Britain, Europe, or the Commonwealth, in addition to her normal round of duties. Her life is a timetable into which meticulous planning has scheduled more calls than anyone would think possible.

This book is a record of some part of the 4000 and more engagements that the Queen has carried out in the years since, on April 21, 1947, in Cape Town, as Princess Elizabeth, she dedicated her life to the service of the Commonwealth.

No sovereign in history has had to shoulder the responsibilities which Queen Elizabeth II now bears. No sovereign has ever had to work so hard. No sovereign has ever more completely fulfilled her promise of service.

S.C.

Contents

Illustrations

Plates in Colour

Plates in Half-tone

I

South to a Dedication

"I DECLARE before you all that my whole life, whether it be long or short, shall be devoted to your service and the service of our great Imperial family to which we all belong, but I shall not have the strength to carry out this resolution alone unless you join in it with me, as I now invite you to do. I know that your support will be unfailingly given." That was the moving dedication of Princess Elizabeth when she broadcast to the world from Cape Town on April 21, 1947.

The plan of a broadcast dedication to service on her twenty-first birthday was Princess Elizabeth's, and it was while the Royal Navy's great battleship H.M.S. *Vanguard* was taking King George VI and Queen Elizabeth and their two daughters to South Africa in February 1947 that she first mentioned the idea to her father. King George gave the matter considerable thought before giving his opinion. It was something that the King had always hoped to hear, but he was anxious not to ask his daughter to take over her vast responsibilities before that was essential. So there were many conversations in the King's day cabin between father and daughter as the great ship thrust southward towards the Cape of Good Hope.

His Majesty realized that Princess Elizabeth had arrived, almost without his having noticed it, at full womanhood.

The laughing girl with the lovely golden hair, wonderful pink-and-white complexion, and beautiful blue eyes had been a child to him throughout the War years. Now she was suggesting a full entry into the world. So, though he was cautiously responsive to her plan, it was with mixed feelings (which were later to be openly expressed at the tomb of Cecil Rhodes in Rhodesia) that he accepted the fact that his elder daughter was now ready to bear some of the burden of one of the world's most difficult jobs.

King George VI had carried a heavy weight of work and decision during the years of the 1939–45 war, and had felt the strain and stress of the Sovereign's life. Throughout those years Princess Elizabeth and Princess Margaret, because they were evacuated to Windsor Castle, had seen less of their parents than they would have done in normal times. The King and Queen had known all too little of their children's childhood.

But during the War years the Princess received help from the perhaps unexpected quarter of the Prime Minister himself. Mr Winston Churchill never forgot that Princess Elizabeth was the future Queen. Whenever they met he made a point of giving her a rapid but concise and skilled résumé of the international situation and the probable future moves of the enemy and the Allies. These talks were invaluable in filling in inevitable gaps in the Princess's general knowledge.

Gradually, as the days on board *Vanguard* passed, the great speech began to take shape, first just pencilled notes —no more than a succession of phrases—little memories of apposite happenings and appropriate quotations: Rupert Brooke's line "Now, God be thanked Who has matched us with His hour"; the saying of William Pitt about England saving herself by her exertions and saving Europe by her example. Many people offered advice and ideas; the importance of the broadcast made it essential that no significant point should be overlooked.

But the driving force behind it all was Princess Elizabeth's will and enthusiasm. She was never tired of suggesting new angles, new phrases.

Those days in the *Vanguard* were thrilling for the young Princess. A congenial crew, a lively, happy ship, and carefree days after the first roughness of the Bay of Biscay made for excitement. Ahead lay the first important tour of her life, the first contact with one of the nations of the Commonwealth. There was also the knowledge that soon after her return from South Africa there was to be the announcement of her engagement to Lieutenant Philip Mountbatten, the twenty-six-year-old naval-officer nephew of Admiral Lord Mountbatten, about which a large part of the world had been speculating for almost eighteen months.

Her friendship with Prince Philip had been something that no one in Court circles had tried to hide. Nor had Princess Elizabeth. What was not so well known was the reason for the repeated denials of a possible engagement between the two. In fact, there were two reasons for withholding the announcement. The first was that both the King and Prince Philip were anxious that the latter's naturalization papers should be completed before any announcement was made, so that Prince Philip could be British in fact as he already was by upbringing and education. Secondly, King George wanted his daughter to have reached her majority and to have taken her full place in the life of the Commonwealth before the question of her marriage was considered. Royal engagements are rarely protracted, and therefore there was no reason to make any announcement until a proper time before the date on which the marriage would take place.

South Africans particularly were curious. At a *braaivleis* (barbecue) in the Orange Free State a member of the Provincial Council could not contain his curiosity, and in the easy informality of the party asked Princess Elizabeth if it were true that she would soon announce her engagement to Prince Philip. The reply was non-committal.

It was not long after *Vanguard* had docked at Cape Town that Princess Elizabeth was able to start her quest for information on South Africa. Field-Marshal Jan Christiaan Smuts ("Oubass"), the veteran Prime Minister of the Union, adopted a grandfatherly attitude to the young Princesses that was typical and touching. Wherever they went together the old man saw to it that the girls were informed of what was going on, its significance and its place in the South African scene. He became the unofficial botanist to the royal party, and on occasions such as the ascent of Table Mountain not only collected bunches of wild flowers for Princess Elizabeth but gravely told her the names of the specimens and their growing habits. "I hope you will not mind an old man's hobbies. I am supposed to be an authority on grasses, but perhaps flowers will prove more interesting to you, and we have such lovely wild flowers in the Cape."

Field-Marshal Smuts, indeed, could name every one of the great variety of wild flowers that grew about Table Mountain and the Cape Peninsula—their botanical names as well as those by which they were more generally known.

There was also the homely Mayor of Cape Town and his wife, Mr and Mrs Abe Bloomberg, who were the hosts to the royal party in the city. They did more than any to give the Princesses an insight into the life and customs of the vast country. In the ballroom of the Cape Town City Hall on February 18, the day after landing, Princess Elizabeth danced several foxtrots and waltzes with the mayor, and found it an ideal opportunity to gain information about the city and the country.

This was a friendship that continued after the end of the tour. When Mr and Mrs Bloomberg went to Britain in October 1947 they were noticed by Princess Margaret when she was naming the new liner *Edinburgh Castle* in the Belfast yard of Harland and Wolff. The Princess said nothing at the time, but the next day a telephone invitation to visit the Royal Family came to the mayor and his wife from Buckingham Palace. There followed several meetings: a visit to the Palace, a theatre visit, and seats in the royal box at the Albert Hall on November 4, 1947.

A young A.D.C. to Field-Marshal Smuts on the South African tour, Major Denis McIldowie, son-in-law of the Prime Minister, also helped to make the tour memorable by his unfailing help with information on every conceivable subject throughout the long and tiring days. The easy informality of the South African welcome, enjoyable though it was, added to the length and fatigue of the functions, but the Royal Family carried off each day with a charm that won every heart—even of the most republican of South Africans. And King George and his family did not forget those who had helped them on the tour. Thus when Major McIldowie and his wife reached London in July 1952 they were surprised to receive an invitation to Buckingham Palace, where they were the guests of Queen Elizabeth and Prince Philip at luncheon. "I did not even know that the Queen knew we were in Britain," said Major McIldowie afterwards. "The invitation came as a complete surprise."

When in March 1947, during the South African tour, the royal party were enjoying a short break at a secluded cove near East London, where Hickman's River flows into the sea, Princess Elizabeth gave further indication of her determination to let nothing stand in the way of her duty to the Commonwealth peoples. It was a hot and blustery day, but down on the beach the breeze was cool and the water delightful. Princess Elizabeth remembered, however, that on the following day she had an important engagement to open the new graving dock at East London. Therefore, while the King and Princess Margaret bathed in the sea, Princess Elizabeth sat down under a canvas awning and drafted her speech. Later, aboard the royal train, she went over the speech and rehearsed it with her sister as her audience.

There was no end to the incidents of that long tour. But one of the most touching, as well as containing its elements of laughter, occurred when the Royal Family were visiting an African reservation. It was a hot day, filled with the oppressive heat of an electric storm, and great, swirling dust-clouds swept continuously across the vast meeting-ground where the royal daïs had been erected. Many thousands of Africans in their traditional dress had gathered to greet their King. The royal party came on to the daïs, tired and dusty, and the loyal Africans leapt to their feet and burst into the national anthem. The King stood at salute and the Queen and the Princesses at attention. At the end of the verse the royal party sank gratefully into their seats. But the loyal crowd wanted to show its loyalty to the full. The second verse of the anthem began, and the royal party came to attention again. Once more the music stopped, and the King and his family sank back in their seats, only to be brought to attention once more by the start of the next verse of *God save the King*. Only one verse had been planned and only one announced, but the Africans decided differently.

Out of the visit to Basutoland on March 12 came the moving story of the leper Guides. Princess Elizabeth and Princess Margaret had inspected 400 Basuto Girl Guides at Maseru Park, near the British Residency. Princess Elizabeth asked if she had reviewed all those present. When told there was one bus-load of leper girls she insisted on being taken to them. With Princess Margaret by her side she walked up to the bus and greeted the leper girls, afterwards walking slowly all round the vehicle so that every one of the girls could see them clearly.

It was actions like these that endeared the whole family to South Africans. Princess Elizabeth and Princess Margaret, perhaps because they were not always in the forefront of affairs, were able to get closer to the ordinary people of the country. And both developed an instinct for making friends which they have never lost. Princess Elizabeth showed, too, a serious side to her nature that had never been apparent in the past.

When on April 15 the Royal Family visited the burial-place of Cecil Rhodes in the Matopo Hills, twenty miles from Bulawayo, in Southern Rhodesia, they climbed a quarter of a mile up the rough, boulder-strewn path from the road. The Queen, in high-heeled shoes, found difficulty in walking over the rough path. Princess Elizabeth, who was wearing low-heeled pumps, took them off and gave them to her mother, who was then able to walk in comfort. The Princess finished the climb barefooted.

At the top King George stood beside the granite slab which marks the grave of Cecil Rhodes. Princess Elizabeth wandered off on her own and stood silently looking out across the desolate bush country of "World's View," the name Rhodes gave to the site. Her father watched her and said to those around him, "Poor Elizabeth. Already she is realizing that she will be alone and lonely all her life; that, no matter who she has by her side, only she can make the final decisions."

Throughout the tour of South Africa Princess Elizabeth continually showed her concern at the terrible winter the people of Britain were having to face with the sub-zero temperatures and the fuel shortages. Her letters home all asked anxiously for news and expressed sympathy with the poor and the lonely who would not be able to afford adequate heating, and stressed how lucky she realized she was to be in sunshine.

The King and Queen and the two Princesses had a tremendous reception from the crowds wherever they appeared after their return home. It was on July 10 that the announcement came from Buckingham Palace. "It is with great pleasure that the King and Queen announce the betrothal of their dearly beloved daughter The Princess Elizabeth to Lieutenant Philip Mountbatten, R.N., son of the late Prince Andrew of Greece and Princess Andrew (Princess Alice of Battenberg), to which the King has gladly given his consent." Immediately after the announcement Princess Elizabeth and Prince Philip drove to Marlborough House to see Queen Mary, and there the Princess's grandmother, who had always hoped that the two young people would want to marry, offered her congratulations. Soon after this visit the Princess and Prince Philip attended a royal garden party in the grounds of Buckingham Palace, and the same evening, at 9.20, appeared on the famous Centre Balcony, to be loudly cheered by a crowd of several thousands massed in front of the Palace. There was no doubt of the popularity of the match with the general public.

Congratulations flowed in from all parts of the world, but one of the most striking came from Mahatma Gandhi. "I send you my blessing and my hopes that your life will be long and happy." Commenting on this message at his weekly prayer meeting, Gandhi said, "You would be foolish to imagine that no Englishman can ever be a friend of India and loyal to her, or that Viscount Mountbatten would not be a servant of the Indian Union because he is of royal blood and because his nephew is going to marry the future Queen of England."

Although there were four months to the wedding, the days became filled with preparation. There was the service itself to be agreed, the dress with its train and veil to be chosen, the bouquet to be selected, the make-up to be used to be decided, and all the going-away and honeymoon clothes to be bought.

Princess Elizabeth was anxious that the ceremony should be notable for its music. She asked Dr William McKie, Australian-born organist of Westminster Abbey, and Dr O. H. Peasgood, the sub-organist, to submit ideas. And she herself went carefully over her own music files to enable her to recall tunes and arrangements which she thought were appropriate. The list of suggestions sent from Westminster Abbey she discussed at length with Prince Philip, and at last the majestic music of the service was decided upon.

The Princess chose as her bridal march the unfamiliar but splendid march by Sir Hubert Parry from his incidental music to *The Birds* of Aristophanes. Her favourite hymn, "Praise, my soul, the King of Heaven," was chosen for the opening processional hymn, and there were old favourites such as Jeremiah Clarke's Trumpet Voluntary and Purcell's Airs on Trumpet Tunes and movements from Handel's Water Music.

When it came to selecting the psalm the Princess had no hesitation in choosing "The Lord is my Shepherd," her favourite, nor, indeed, the setting "Crimond." Princess Elizabeth remembered a descant which she wished to include in the setting, and told Dr McKie that she had heard it in Scotland. No copy could be found, but the Princess sang it to Dr McKie, who wrote it in manuscript. It was then found that the composer was Dr W. Baird Ross of Stirling, who wrote the work for George Watson's Ladies' College in 1929.

The first sketches for the dress were submitted by Hartnell, and Princess Elizabeth—after many consultations with her mother, the Queen, and with Princess Margaret—made her choice out of twelve designs. The final choice was of pearl-coloured slipper satin embroidered in crystals and pearls, with a heart-shaped neckline and long, tight sleeves, fitting bodice with pointed waistline, and full, ground-length skirt. The embroidery was of garlands of roses in raised pearls, ears of corn in crystals and drop-pearls; tulle star-flowers and orange-blossoms were appliquéd to the satin and bordered with seed pearls and crystals. The train had three layers of tulle, fifteen feet long and fastened to the shoulders. Satin star-flowers were appliquéd to the tulle with the same type of pearl and crystal embroidery as for the dress.

The engagement ring was made in the workshops of Philip Antrobus, of Regent Place, London. The ring of platinum was set with eleven diamonds—a central stone of three carats (the size of a little-finger nail) and five small diamonds on either side. The stones were provided by

Princess Andrew of Greece, Prince Philip's mother, who brought one of her own rings to the jewellers and herself suggested the form of design the new ring should take. Mr George Taubl made the ring, and Mr Harry Marchant set the stones.

The wedding-ring was made in the workshop of Mr W. Bertolle, a West End jeweller, from the same gold nugget from which Princess Elizabeth's mother's ring was made —gold mined in the Welsh hills.

Princess Elizabeth and Prince Philip spent many hours deciding who should figure among the 2000 guests at the wedding. There were few official guests, and most of those invited were personal friends of the young couple or those who had performed some service for them in the past. To the outside world there were surprises, but all the names gave evidence of the thought that had been given to the list. One was Miss Mabel Syanden, who had helped to make the silk for the wedding-dress. There were also twenty girls from the workrooms where the wedding clothes had been made. Eighty-year-old Miss M. J. Crewe, once nurse to Prince Philip, was another guest, as was Mrs Cobina Wright, an American who had sent the Prince parcels and cheery letters during the War. The royal riding instructors were invited; also the stationmaster at Wolferton Station, the station for Sandringham, and the schoolmistress of Birkhall, in Scotland. The list was compiled from letter files, from diaries, from conversations about past meetings. Princess Elizabeth and Prince Philip would talk over the list at tea-time. As names came to mind they would discuss whether they should be added to a list which could have reached many thousands but had, in fact, to be restricted to a few hundreds.

So many wedding gifts were received from all over the

world that a decision had to be made whether to accept them. Normally they would have been sent back with a letter regretting that no member of the Royal Family could accept gifts except from a personal friend. But King George was so touched by this obvious affection for his daughter and her future husband that he decided to make an exception in this case. As soon as she heard this Princess Elizabeth thought of the idea of inviting all who had sent presents to attend a reception at St James's Palace, where she could meet them and they could see all the presents set out.

The Princess now had her own household. Her engagements were being arranged separately from those of the King and Queen, and there were other signs that she was to take over more and more of the work of everyday contact with the people from her father.

And so the crowded days led to the eve-of-the-wedding party at Buckingham Palace, where a radiant Princess Elizabeth, in a gown of tulle embroidered with gold paillettes, and wearing the necklace of twenty-one diamonds which had been South Africa's twenty-first-birthday gift, met many of those who were to be in Westminster Abbey on the following day for the marriage ceremony itself. The Princess met Mr Winston Churchill as she passed through the State rooms with Prince Philip. As they paused to shake his hand the great statesman reminded them that he remembered the weddings of the Princess's grandfather and grandmother and also of her father and mother.

Twenty-four hours before the ceremony King George made Lieutenant Philip Mountbatten a Knight of the Garter and conferred on him the titles of "His Royal Highness Duke of Edinburgh and Baron Greenwich and Earl of Merioneth."

In her consultations with the Archbishop of Canterbury about the actual order of the wedding service Princess Elizabeth insisted that the old and traditional form be used, which included the promise "to obey him, serve him, love, honour and keep him in sickness and in health." When this became known there was considerable surprise and some controversy in the country. In fact, her decision was in keeping with her beliefs. Princess Elizabeth had always believed that the principle of the husband being the head of the family is the only guarantee of happiness in the home. Even as Queen she has never wavered in this belief, and her own complete happiness is a result.

2

La Petite Souris

It had been planned that Princess Elizabeth and Prince Philip should live at Sunninghill Park, the lovely house near Ascot, in Berkshire, and comfortably near to Windsor, which they had bought from Mr and Mrs Philip Hill. But while the Court was at Balmoral in August 1947 the young couple had received the news that the house had been completely gutted by fire and that there was no hope of its being restored.

There were immediately rumours that the fire had been sabotage and that political interests were responsible. But Princess Elizabeth would have none of this. Nor, indeed, would the experts who investigated the fire.

When it was decided that after their wedding the Princess and Prince Philip must live at Buckingham Palace the situation was not without significance. Princess Elizabeth and her husband were living with Father and Mother, a condition which was repeated in many thousands of homes throughout the country. Vast though Buckingham Palace is, and interminable as are its corridors and State rooms, the royal apartments are not really designed to provide an ideal lay-out for separate families which are carrying out full-scale royal engagement lists, with all the intricate planning that that entails. The royal apartments take up only a very small part of Buckingham Palace, and Princess

Elizabeth and her husband in fact lived in the small group of rooms that had been the Princess's before her marriage. They took Windlesham Moor, near Windsor, as a week-end home.

At the start of 1948 Prince Philip was at work in his new temporary job at the Admiralty, and Princess Elizabeth got into the habit of seeing him off to work each day when, soon after half-past eight, he walked out through the great Palace gates and along the Mall towards the looming Admiralty Arch. And she was also often at a window overlooking the courtyard to watch him come home again in the early evening. Then over tea in their sitting-room they would discuss the events of the day, often preparatory to getting dressed to go out together to some official function. The Princess was taking on more and more public work.

There was an unusual function for the young couple on March 3, when they drove down to the London Docks and went aboard the sailing-ship *Pamir* in Shadwell Basin. This famous barque, which was one of the last of the square-rigged sailing-ships in commission in the world, was a training-ship for New Zealand officers and men. The Princess and Prince Philip had tea on board. Prince Philip went all round the ship and examined the standing and running gear with expert eyes. "I would like nothing more when I go to sea again than to make a trip in sail," Philip told members of the crew, thus revealing that his shore job at the Admiralty was intended to be only temporary. "He showed a remarkable knowledge of sailing-ships. We all think he is a good 'square-rigged' man who has gone 'turbine-minded,'" said Captain Collier, the *Pamir*'s master. *Pamir*, a four-masted barque, foundered in a North Atlantic hurricane on September 22, 1957, with the loss of eighty lives. She was then owned and operated by the German shipping firm of Zerssen and Company, of Hamburg, having been sold by New Zealand in 1951.

But the royal engagements were not all as lighthearted as this. On April 12 the Princess and Prince Philip attended the unveiling of the statue in Grosvenor Square, London, of the war-time President of the United States, Franklin D. Roosevelt. Mrs Roosevelt, the widow of the famous President, was there to pull the cords that released the flags shrouding the twelve-foot statue in bronze.

Princess Elizabeth never met President Roosevelt, but she found Mrs Roosevelt an eager biographer. The Princess had met the President's wife during the War both at Buckingham Palace and at Windsor. They had much to remember of those war-time days, and laughingly recalled the occasion when Mrs Roosevelt went to Windsor to see the King and Queen once more before setting out for home. The President's wife arrived at the Castle suffering from a bad head cold. Handkerchief to nose, she began to apologize to the King, only to find that he himself had an equally bad cold. Their conversation was carried on largely through handkerchiefs.

On this 1948 visit Mrs Roosevelt was able to help in the matter of information on the United States against the time when a visit to the United States would be made by Princess Elizabeth. Although nothing had then been arranged, the Princess had already discussed with her father the possibility of a visit to Canada and the United States. She seized the opportunity of Mrs Roosevelt's visit to enlarge her knowledge of life in North America.

Sir William Reid Dick, the famous Scottish sculptor, was the creator of the Roosevelt statue. Princess Elizabeth knew him well, and had, in fact, sat to him in his studio in Maida Vale (once the workroom of Alfred Gilbert, the creator of Eros in Piccadilly Circus). The sculptor had carved the recumbent figure of King George V for St George's Chapel, Windsor, and had also produced the effigy of Queen Mary, in full regalia of a Lady of the Order of the Garter, to await the time of her own death and burial in St George's Chapel. This, at first sight, somewhat ghoulish practice is always followed in cases where a sovereign predeceases his wife, and Queen Mary gave sittings to Sir William with complete unconcern about their meaning.

When Princess Elizabeth met Sir William Reid Dick at the Roosevelt Memorial ceremony she already knew that she would be meeting him again at Buckingham Palace in July to present him with the Albert Medal of the Royal Society of Arts, first sculptor ever to win the award. "Your statues of my grandfather, King George V, and of President Roosevelt have been widely proclaimed for their artistic merit," she told him then. "On the rim of the medal you will find the legend 'For national memories in living stone.' Your skill has helped us to keep those memories fresh and fair."

On May 22, 1948, the Princess visited Coventry to open the new Central Square, and there saw an open space left for one of Sir William's more controversial works, the statue of Lady Godiva making her famous ride. The statue had still not been set up when the Princess reached the city.

But before she visited the Midlands the Princess and Prince Philip undertook an official visit to Paris, where their welcome from the vast crowds was so moving that as they drove down the Champs-Élysées after visiting the Unknown Soldier's Tomb under the Arc de Triomphe onlookers could see the tears in Princess Elizabeth's eyes and on her cheeks. At the Élysée Palace, President Auriol of France presented the Princess with the Grand Cross of the Legion of Honour, and then said, "The Protocol demands that I should salute you with the accolade [a kiss on both cheeks], but I delegate my powers to your husband." Ten years later President Auriol's successor was to address Princess Elizabeth (then the Queen) in almost the same words in presenting the Legion of Honour to Prince Philip, "Et maintenant, Madame, l'accolade."

Princess Elizabeth and Prince Philip visited Longchamps races on the following Sunday, and Prince Philip won 1000 francs on the totalizator by backing a horse which ran third. Later the young couple dined in the famous Tour d'Argent in the Latin Quarter, and from there went on to one of the city's smartest night clubs, Chez Carrère, in the Rue Pierre Charron.

"La petite souris," as the Princess was called by Parisians as a tribute to her shyness, came home to face some criticism, particularly from the Free Church of Scotland, for attending races, a restaurant, and a night club on a Sunday. It did not matter that the Princess, when asked to sanction the programme before her departure, had accepted only because her hosts had arranged a schedule in keeping with their own ways of life. The French Home Office issued a statement: "We in Paris loved Princess Elizabeth because she became *tout à fait* Parisienne. Visiting another country it is necessary to be like the citizens of that country."

But there were even more who sprang to the defence of the Princess and her husband and who pointed out that they had twice been to church on that very Sunday. Yet it was the first occasion on which Princess Elizabeth had

had the truth of her father's remarks in Rhodesia that "she will be lonely all her life" so plainly brought home to her. Now she had had abundant evidence of the fact that her every act was watched and that there were some who would always be ready to complain and to criticize.

It had been openly stated in Paris during her visit that Princess Elizabeth was expecting a baby in November. Now the people of Britain began to discuss the same possibility. But the Princess continued with her engagements. She visited Coventry, received a degree at Oxford and the freedom of the City of Cardiff, visited the Bath and West Show, inspected the 3rd Battalion, Grenadier Guards, and attended the First Guards Club dinner during the course of one week at the end of May after her return from Paris.

On the last day of May Princess Elizabeth, as President of the Royal Society of Arts, attended the first meeting of the Council to mark the centenary of the Great Exhibition of 1851. Princess Elizabeth has always had a special interest in the work of her great-great-grandfather, Prince Albert the Prince Consort, and with some reason. She could not overlook the fact that she herself was in an identical position to Queen Victoria in the matter of the succession to the throne, nor that Prince Philip must one day, in the normal course of events, stand in a similar position to the Prince Consort.

Prince Albert had been the driving force behind the 1851 Exhibition. Queen Victoria described the Exhibition as "a fairy scene." "Albert's dearest memory is immortalized in this great conception," the Queen added. And Princess Elizabeth was aware that her husband was already becoming known as a man who realized the vital part science must play in the British economy and was prepared to work to encourage the development of technology in every field of industry.

"I hope that in emphasizing our achievements of the past and present you will stress no less sharply our responsibilities to the future. Then the Festival of Britain in 1951 may prove to be not simply an end in itself but a beginning of many good things, and it may be an event which, by its excellence, permanently raises the regard in which British artists, scientists, craftsmen, and technicians are held," she said to the Council.

After that meeting Princess Elizabeth and Prince Philip were often active behind the scenes, encouraging progress and suggesting ideas for inclusion in the South Bank Festival.

There were to be very few other public engagements in 1948 for Princess Elizabeth. Prince Philip took over an increasing share of the diary items. The Princess worked throughout June and July, although her last public engagement was at the Queen Elizabeth Hospital for Children at Banstead, in Surrey, in June. Before that she had driven in state through the City of London on June 8 to be present when Prince Philip became a Freeman of the City. There she heard her husband make a dedication to service which almost matched her own: "The ideal that my wife and I have set before us is to make the utmost use of the special opportunities we have to try to bring home to our generation the full importance of that contribution and the effort, both at work and play, that is required of us," he said.

The Princess also attended the annual general meeting of the Shaftesbury Homes at the Albert Hall and presented Queen Mary's prizes, and saw the Metropolitan Police Horse Show at Imber Court. But an announcement that she would retire temporarily from public life at the end of the month prepared the people for the announcement of the forthcoming birth of her child. In fact, she did attend the sitting of the House of Lords at which Prince Philip took his seat supported by the Dukes of Norfolk and Beaufort. She also received Commander Collins, R.N., at Buckingham Palace, when he presented her with the lamp from which the Olympic torch had been lit in Greece before it set off on its journey to England.

Prince Philip, with almost daily engagements, showed his keen interest in a great variety of national interests—sport, industry, the City Livery Companies. His speeches (all written by himself) were models of their kind—witty, cheerful, and to the point. Prince Philip could easily have taken a line of 'sitting on the fence' in his speeches. Instead he made no speech unless he had some contribution to make for the function concerned, yet his positive approach evoked surprisingly little criticism from any source. Indeed, he was almost everywhere welcomed as a young man who "has a mind of his own and is not afraid to exercise it."

During the spring and summer Princess Elizabeth and Prince Philip had made themselves familiar with the political scene in a way that could not possibly cause offence to even the greatest stickler for conformity. On April 15 they dined at 10 Downing Street with the Prime Minister and Mrs Attlee. After dinner their conversation was of politics and diplomacy; of the Commonwealth and the advancement of the colonies. Here was a chance for informal talks with Ministers that the Princess could rarely enjoy. So it was an additional pleasure to be able to dine on May 11 with the Chancellor of the Exchequer and Lady Cripps, when they were able to discuss the struggle that the country was having to achieve stability preparatory to moving forward in the economic field.

These were new departures in royal relations with the Government in power. They showed that Princess Elizabeth and her husband were fully alive to the changes that had come over Britain and the Commonwealth and were anxious that they should lose no opportunity of fitting themselves into the new pattern so that they could give the best service to the community.

Princess Elizabeth had visited children's courts—further evidence of her desire to learn about the everyday life of the country and to get first-hand information on the seamy side as well as on the more ordered circle in which she habitually moved.

By October the whole country and a large part of the world were becoming interested in the approaching royal birth. Princess Elizabeth, although she was not undertaking public engagements, was not idle. She herself selected the nurses who were to have charge of her and her baby. Sister Helen Rowe was in charge before the birth, and moved into Buckingham Palace ten days before it took place.

Princess Elizabeth chose for the nursery the room which she herself had had as a baby of nine months. It is on the second floor facing south. Princess Elizabeth had slept in this room with her nurse when her father and mother, as Duke and Duchess of York, had travelled to Australia in January 1927. Later the room had been her schoolroom.

As under-nurse Princess Elizabeth chose Miss Mabel Anderson, of Elgin, Scotland.

The nursery was equipped with the cot that had been Princess Elizabeth's from the time she was born at 17 Bruton Street, a frilled, canopied cot in peach satin and

At Balmoral the Queen can usually enjoy a carefree holiday, and although the crowds still gather to greet her there, as this picture taken at Crathie shows, she is among her 'ain folk' and can really relax.

The royal progress through Canada in 1951 was at times almost a 'whistle-stop' tour. Princess Elizabeth and Prince Philip usually waved their "Good-byes" from the observation platform of the last coach of the train. Here they are saying farewell to Rivière du Loup, in Quebec Province.

The days were often hot and tiring for the young princesses during the tour of South Africa made with King George VI and Queen Elizabeth in 1947, but pony-riding beside the sea helped create a cool breeze. In this picture Princess Elizabeth and Princess Margaret are cantering on the beach at Bonza Bay, East London.

cream net. Princess Margaret had also slept in it. There was a cradle with a draped head-curtain trimmed in peach satin, covered in cream net. There was a wickerwork Moses cot trimmed with ivory satin which Queen Mary provided. That also had been used to carry both Princess Elizabeth and Princess Margaret from their nursery to their mother's room. A baby's toilet hamper, likewise trimmed with ivory satin, was also part of the nursery equipment.

Princess Elizabeth chose all of the baby's clothing. There were fifty-five garments in the layette, and the garments were all made by twenty-five retired dressmakers and drapery-store assistants from the Cottage Homes for the Aged administered by the Linen and Woollen Draper's Institution, of which Princess Elizabeth was patron and in whose work she had always taken a keen interest.

On November 10 the Princess went to the pictures, to the surprise of every one, but it was in Sir Alexander Korda's private cinema in the film magnate's Piccadilly home. The previous day she had telephoned from the Palace to say that she would like to see a film by Burgess Meredith, and this was arranged for the party, which consisted of the Princess, Prince Philip, and Princess Margaret.

The world heard the news of the birth of a prince on the evening of November 14. The birth had taken place in the Princess's own room, and a break with precedent was that on this occasion there was no Home Secretary waiting in an adjoining room. Instead King George telephoned the news to Mr Chuter Ede.

On December 15 Prince Charles Philip Arthur George was christened in the Music Room of the Palace. In the lofty, bow-shaped room with its eighteen columns of blue, which contrast with the ivory and gold of the walls, the font was placed on a platform of crimson velvet.

Christmas roses, white narcissi, white carnations, white heather, freesias, and myrtle (grown from sprays used at Princess Elizabeth's wedding), with grape hyacinths and forget-me-nots to provide the 'blue for a boy' motif, formed the floral decorations. Two hymns, chosen by Princess Elizabeth, were sung: "Holy, Holy, Holy," and "Oh, worship the King."

When Sister Helen Rowe had completed her work at the Palace she was replaced by Miss Helen Lightbody, henceforth to be the nanny of the royal children.

3

Clarence House

KING GEORGE was already a sick man when Prince Charles was born on November 14, 1948. Princess Elizabeth had many times joined her mother in urging that the King should give up some of his duties in order to get more rest. But there was no trait in the character of King George more strongly developed than his determination to let nothing stand in the way of his service to the Commonwealth. And his daughter, cast in the same mould, found it hard, even though she feared for her father, to refer too frequently to the subject of rest.

When it was announced on November 23 that the projected visit of the King and Queen to Australia must be cancelled there was considerable alarm, which was not completely allayed by the announcement that, although the King was suffering from an obstruction to the circulation through the arteries of his legs, "His Majesty's general health, including the condition of his heart, gives no reason for concern."

The cancellation of all the King's engagements meant that a greater number must be carried by the other members of the Royal Family, and Princess Elizabeth and Prince Philip took over many of these. The Princess herself suffered an attack of measles while she was at Sandringham in January, but as she had no important public engagements until the first day of March it was possible for her to allow the illness to take its course and to enjoy the proper period of convalescence. She stayed in her own room at Sandringham, and for the few days during which there was any danger of infection—although it is rare that small babies catch the disease—Prince Charles was separated from his mother.

On March 1 the Princess and Prince Philip set off for Scotland on the first of a series of tours which were to take up a great part of 1949. They were in no doubt about the state of the King's health, and realized that the full extent of his illness had been kept from the public in order that there should be no adverse economic effects through concern for the King's health. The cancellation of the King's tour of Australia had involved insurance claims estimated at £250,000, and the King realized only too well that public anxiety over the Sovereign's health can have a big and adverse effect on business generally.

So Princess Elizabeth and Prince Philip, although they knew that the King was to undergo an operation soon after their return to London, gave no sign of their anxiety as they carried out their engagements in Edinburgh. But every night, from the Palace of Holyroodhouse, Princess Elizabeth telephoned her father and mother at Buckingham Palace for the latest news.

The King was present on March 4 when the deputation of Privy Councillors from the House of Lords came to Buckingham Palace to present an address of congratulations on the birth of Prince Charles. His Majesty waited in the Bow Room for a similar deputation of House of Commons Privy Councillors which followed an hour later. But the members of both parties noted the pallor of the King's cheeks and his obvious pain when moving. He sat throughout the ceremonies.

On March 11, only a few hours before his operation, King George received in audience the Right Hon. H. V. Evatt, Minister for External Affairs and Deputy Prime Minister of Australia. On the following morning at ten o'clock at Buckingham Palace the doctors performed the operation of lumbar sympathectomy on the King's right side. It was successful, and the King, according to his doctors, immediately began to make a normal recovery.

The other members of the Royal Family continued with their engagements as usual. The Queen opened a block of flats in St John's Wood, London, and the same evening went with Princess Elizabeth and Prince Philip to see Ibsen's *Wild Duck* at St Martin's Theatre. Princess Margaret with a party of friends saw *Harvey* at the Prince of Wales Theatre. It was all so calm and reassuring.

Princess Elizabeth, in fact, lost no opportunity of allaying public alarm. When she visited the headquarters of the Women's Voluntary Service on March 24 to make a draw for blankets for mothers who had had children on the same day as the birth of Prince Charles she announced that King George was "getting on very well indeed."

On March 30, however, the King's doctors announced that "we have advised His Majesty that a prolonged period of convalescence will be necessary." That revealed to some the danger to King George's health. Twelve years of continued strain and nervous tension had taken their toll of a constitution which had never been robust, but which had been worked to the maximum in the interests of the Commonwealth.

About this time the Princess and Prince Philip began to make short visits to see how work was proceeding on

Clarence House, their chosen London home. The Government had voted £50,000 for its repair and rehabilitation in 1948, but allegations that this sum had been vastly exceeded—one report quoted the enormous figure of £250,000—were made.

The Government denied the allegations. "It is unlikely that the amount spent will exceed the estimate by more than ten per cent.," declared the Ministry of Works before completion of the work. Mr Norman Kennedy, secretary of the London District Committee of the Amalgamated Society of Woodworkers, refused to accept these denials. He declared that he had challenged Princess Elizabeth and Prince Philip on the cost of alterations to the house and was "waiting for a call from Buckingham Palace to go and talk the matter over."

The call did not come. But, as no one had expected that it would, there was no tendency to believe that the silence meant that in fact a quarter of a million had been spent on the house. Rather it was reckoned that a figure of something over £60,000 was correct. The Minister of Works announced that £50,000 had been spent on alterations, but there were also other works, costing between £5000 and £8000, designed to improve the comfort of the great house.

A great deal of the apparent expenditure seen by the various workmen in the house was, in fact, not the responsibility either of the Ministry of Works or of the Princess and her husband. The woods on which so many of the members of the Amalgamated Society of Woodworkers demonstrated their skill were largely wedding gifts from Canadian and Australian organizations. The furnishings, which in some cases gave rise to extraordinary stories relative to their magnificence, were also largely wedding gifts from municipalities in Great Britain.

Princess Elizabeth's rooms were on the first floor. Her bedroom overlooked St James's Park and was furnished with a rosewood suite. Much of the additional furniture she had had at Buckingham Palace. The hangings were of red rose and cream carried out in heavy satin. The walls were in rose-pink.

Next door was Prince Philip's bed-dressing-room—a gift of the City of Glasgow, and designed after consultation with the Prince by the well-known Scottish designer Neil Morris. The room had fourteen pieces of furniture, including a divan bed fitted into a recess, wall-bookshelves, and writing-desk. The walls were lined with Scottish white sycamore, the wood chosen for the furniture. There were hidden cupboards in the walls. In the Prince's study on the ground floor the plain waxed Canadian maplewood wainscoting was a gift from the Canadian Pacific Railway.

The Lancaster Room, one of the main reception rooms, was the gift of the people of Lancashire. The alabaster lighting bowl, containing sixteen lamps and said to be the largest in Britain, which hung in the library on the ground floor, was also a wedding gift.

In fact, Clarence House is fitted with old-fashioned sash-corded windows, which, by direct order of Princess Elizabeth, were not replaced, on the grounds that to replace them would be to incur unnecessary expense.

But, unsubstantiated though the criticisms of extravagance were, they were not ignored by the Royal Family. The King was always anxious that there should be no opportunity for the few to make political capital out of any real or supposed privilege of the Royal Family, and Princess Elizabeth had always attempted to keep that fine balance between the need to maintain pageantry and the necessity to observe economy. It is a task that is as thankless as it is difficult.

Princess Elizabeth and Prince Philip visited Lancashire at the end ot March, and this tour was followed on April 28 by a visit to Wales. On May 25 they flew to Belfast. Back home Princess Elizabeth took the Trooping the Colour ceremony on Horse Guards Parade on June 9 on behalf of her father, and on June 21 left with Prince Philip in H.M.S. *Anson* for a tour of the Channel Islands. In all of these tours the young couple revealed that friendly touch which has since endeared them to the ordinary people in every part of the world.

There can never be any 'rules' for royal decisions on accepting public engagements. Every day the sovereign must choose one or two engagements out of a list which averages fifty requests daily throughout the year. It is inevitable that many people must feel overlooked. Princess Elizabeth, on those first tours of her public life, showed a sure appreciation for the things which would give the greatest pleasure to the greatest number. Yet there were also many small, friendly, and personal gestures that might never have been known. On the tour of Wales no one knew that Princess Elizabeth was looking out for a woman who had written to say she would be waving to the royal car as it passed through Barmouth, in Merionethshire.

"I wrote to the Princess and told her I would be waving a big red-white-and-blue rosette as she went through Barmouth, and in reply I had a letter saying she would look out for me," said Mrs F. M. Allday. "I went to a hill on the road from Barmouth, in Dolgelly, where I knew she would pass in her car. When the royal car came along I waved my rosette and the Princess saw me. The car stopped, and I had a chat with the Princess for quite three or four minutes.

"My married daughter was there with my grandson. The Princess took the baby in her arms and said, 'What a fine baby he is.'"

A little interlude on a quiet country road, a kindly gesture that put the royal schedule five minutes behind time and gave pleasure only to the three people who knew of it. Yet that sort of incident was repeated many times during the summer of 1949.

All through June and July the Princess and her husband toured Britain—Macclesfield (immediately after the Channel Islands visit), Derby, Nottingham (for the quincentenary celebrations), Mansfield, Shrewsbury, the West Riding of Yorkshire. But in between—on July 4—they went into residence at Clarence House with no more publicity than the issue of their first Court Circular from the house. At 2 P.M. the personal standard of the Princess was broken at the flagstaff on the roof when the Princess arrived from Windlesham Moor, and at the same moment sentries of the Welsh Guards took up their posts at the gates.

August and September were holiday months, but they had a greater importance for the Princess and Prince Philip than normally, for on October 12 the Prince was to resume his seagoing career with a posting as First Lieutenant in H.M.S. *Chequers*. The Prince had had a most difficult period in which he had attempted to fulfil his naval duties and yet undertake a large number of royal engagements. It was a dual rôle which, besides involving some considerable strain for the Prince, also brought him in for a small amount of ill-mannered criticism on the grounds that he would be obtaining promotion in the Royal Navy without earning it. In fact—in the same way as his uncle, Lord

Mountbatten—Prince Philip was promoted in strict sequence and only after passing his promotion examinations exactly as other naval officers.

With her husband away in the Mediterranean Princess Elizabeth had important public engagements to fulfil almost every day. But one at least brought her world attention in a way which she may not have anticipated before the event. On October 18 the Princess addressed 2000 mothers at the young wives' rally of the Mothers' Union at the Central Hall, Westminster. "We live in an age of growing self-indulgence, of hardening materialism, and of falling moral standards," she said. "Some of the very principles on which the family, and therefore the health of the nation, is founded are in danger. But the young members of the Mothers' Union, who now have two thousand branches in Britain, are a powerful force on the right side.

"One of your first objects is to uphold the sanctity of marriage. There will, of course, always be unhappy marriages, especially when, as in time of war, it is so difficult for people to live normal married lives.

"But when we see around us the havoc which has been wrought, above all among the children, by the break-up of homes we can have no doubt that divorce and separation are responsible for some of the darkest evil in our society to-day."

The relationship of husband and wife was a permanent one, said the Princess. Nobody had a greater responsibility in life than a mother, but there were many who needed guidance and wise counsel. A child learned by example. It was important to see not only that the children said their prayers, but also that parents practised Christianity in their own lives. "We surely cannot expect our children to do what we are too lazy to do ourselves," said the Princess.

"I believe there is a great fear in our generation of being labelled priggish. In consequence people are sometimes afraid to show disapproval of what they know to be wrong, and thus they end by seeming to condone what in their hearts they dislike. It is just as wrong to err on that side as it is to be intolerant and over-critical."

This was one of the most outspoken royal speeches for years. The response from all parts of the world was immediate. Religious and women's group leaders in Canada, Australia, and New Zealand welcomed the Princess's statements. In the U.S.A. the *New York Herald Tribune* declared:

"We like to think she showed a very human unwillingness to stay within the bounds of the merely gracious and formal speech that British tradition imposes on royalty.

"She spoke, as might any serious young leader who finds all is not right with the world, of divorce rate and evils that attend broken homes.

"It takes a woman with a far more than normal poise, courage, and independent mind to emerge as a distinct, let alone decisive, personality from the rôle prescribed for a Princess in Britain's almost entirely symbolic royalty," the newspaper declared.

There were inevitable adverse criticisms. Mr Robert Pollard, Chairman of the Marriage Law Reform Committee, said, "We have observed with regret the statement of Princess Elizabeth. Divorce and separation are not themselves responsible for the evils to which she refers. It is the causes, such as inadequate housing and unstable partners, which lead to the break-up of marriages.

"Divorce only recognizes in law an existing state of

facts that a marriage has failed. The harm to children can be greater in a home where both parents are at loggerheads than if divorce ensues," claimed Mr Pollard.

While argument and counter-argument were building up around her the Princess was visiting Exeter and the Duchy of Cornwall and Plymouth. She would have been less than human if she had not sometimes wondered during that day if she had not committed an error of judgment and unwittingly called down on the Mothers' Union such allegations as "it has been notorious for years for its opposition to any amendment of the divorce law."

But King George and Queen Elizabeth were completely satisfied that their daughter had been right, for their views on marriage and family life were the same. Princess Elizabeth had shown to the world that she had ideas and a will of her own, and in the volume of approval of her words the few disparaging voices were almost unnoticeable.

On October 24 the Princess, with Princess Margaret, visited the House of Commons for the debate on economy cuts to be made by Mr Attlee's Government. The Princess joined in the laughter when a question to Mr Herbert Morrison, Lord President of the Council, about the use of vitamin E for heart trouble caused Colonel Gomme-Duncan (Conservative, Perth) to ask if there could be an issue to members about 3.30 P.M.

The Princesses went to the House in view of the importance of the occasion. Princess Elizabeth had suggested the visit as it seemed likely to provide a real insight into the state of the country's finances and the plans of the Government to overcome the difficulties.

After a short visit to Stoke-on-Trent and the Potteries Princess Elizabeth prepared for a short holiday in Malta. Prince Charles was left at Windlesham Moor with Nurse

Lightbody, and on November 20 the Princess flew from London Airport in a Viking aircraft of the King's Flight.

In Malta, for her stay of a week, she lived at the Villa Guardamangia, the official residence of Admiral Lord Mountbatten, Commander-in-Chief, Mediterranean, and at every opportunity she spent her days in the same pursuits and pastimes as any other naval officer's wife in Malta.

4

When in Rome

PRINCESS ELIZABETH began her public duties in 1950 with a visit on January 25 to Crawley New Town. There was a personal reason for this visit, the first to be paid to any of the New Towns by a member of the Royal Family. The Princess had followed from the outset the Government plan for the dispersal and redistribution of the population of London and other great cities. It had appealed to her as an imaginative approach to a problem made more urgent and imperative by the lessons of the war-time bombing. She was convinced that thinning out of overcrowding was essential from a safety as well as from a social point of view.

She had listened to the debate in the House of Commons in October 1949 when Mr Attlee had had to outline economy cuts, and had realized that the cuts in capital expenditure and housing must materially affect the progress of the New Town development. Thus she eagerly accepted the invitation to go to Crawley to name a new main road through the industrial area and to plant a maple-tree to commemorate the war-time association between the town and the Canadian Army. The visit enabled her to see what progress was being made in the building and also to forge one more link between Britain and a country of the Commonwealth.

What she saw in Crawley gave Princess Elizabeth a complete understanding of the difficulties which need to be overcome in the transference of thousands of families from settled environments into quite different surroundings. She talked with workmen and some of the new inhabitants whose lives had been spent in the crowded conditions of London and to whom green fields and wooded copses were a thrilling experience.

This was a further step in the Princess's political education. From the days of her youth she had taken a keen interest in politics, recognizing their importance in the life of the sovereign. Isolated from political activity though she was, she could see no reason to be similarly isolated from political thought, and she realized that her future position would demand that she should be well informed on the policies and plans of all the main political parties. As Queen Elizabeth II, indeed, she is regarded at Westminster as the best-informed political observer in the country, with a shrewd and incisive appreciation of all the differing aims of the political parties.

The sovereign always keeps in the closest touch, not only with the Government of the day by means of the weekly meeting with the Prime Minister and by regular talks with other Cabinet Ministers, but also, through secretaries and other officials of the Royal Household, with the work and ideas of the official Opposition and other parties.

On May 10, 1950, Princess Elizabeth dined with the Speaker of the House of Commons at Speakers' House, Westminster, and in the party were twenty-nine M.P.'s of the main political parties. This was the first occasion on which an Heir to the Throne had ever dined officially with the Speaker in his house. The after-dinner conversation was described by one guest as a brilliant condensation of a year of debate into an hour of conversation. Internal politics, foreign affairs, and future trends all came under discussion.

There is something symbolic in the occasional meeting between a member of the Royal Family and the First Commoner of the Kingdom. Both must be strictly impartial in a political sense—the one without any official contact with the House of Commons, the other closely involved in every debate in the House.

During February and March 1950 Princess Elizabeth had had a varied list of engagements, which ranged from a visit to the Honourable Company of Master Mariners aboard H.M.S. *Wellington* by the Thames Embankment on February 7 to presenting prizes at the London Chamber of Commerce Prize Distribution at the Guildhall. Between March 2 and March 4, she visited Bath, Bristol, and the Severn Wild Fowl Trust, and was back in London for the visit of the President of France and Mme Auriol on March 7. President Auriol and his wife made a great impression on London, and they also went back to France with the warmest memories of their stay. But perhaps the most important single achievement of the visit was the real friendship that developed between the visitors and the Royal Family.

There was nothing of diplomatic 'friendliness' about the contacts of the two families. Mme Auriol particularly became the firmest of friends with Princess Elizabeth, and Mme Auriol and the President spent many happy moments playing with Prince Charles. Mme Auriol nursed the baby several times during their stay at the Palace, and the President admitted afterwards, "Unlike most babies, especially little boys, he was not shy, but took at once to Mme Auriol

Though she was an expert in the dances of Britain, it was not until her tour of Canada in 1951 that Princess Elizabeth learned the exhilarating movements of the square dance. Here she is seen in flower-patterned dirndl skirt and brown-checked blouse dancing at the party given by the Governor-General, Field-Marshal Viscount Alexander, at Rideau Hall, Ottawa.

With Sir Philip Mitchell, then Governor of Kenya, in attendance, the Queen (she was still Princess Elizabeth at the time) carries out an engagement in Kenya during the ill-fated tour of the Commonwealth in 1952 which was cut short by the death of King George VI.

and smiled at her. He seemed a little taken aback when he first saw me, but we became firm friends."

Among the colourful functions of the French President's visit was a banquet at the French Embassy in Kensington Palace Gardens for the King and Queen and Princess Elizabeth. The 400 guests were received in the salon, with its curtains of pale blue, Louis XV furnishings, and its magnificent Savonnerie carpet of the Louis XIV period. Servants from the Élysée Palace in Paris in their traditional livery served the meal on the famous Sèvres china, which had been specially brought to London.

The Princess wore a robe of stiff white satin, with a bodice cut with a low, square neckline, softened by two folds of satin. Her skirt was stiffened with a lattice-work design of raised white satin. She wore the red ribbon of the Grand Cordon of the Legion of Honour and, almost unnoticed, for the first time in public, the magnificent ruby-and-diamond necklace which had been her wedding present from her mother and father. The necklace has a mounting in gold and is regarded as a fine example of bandeau setting. Her tiara was formed of diamond-encrusted fleurs-de-lis, matching a diamond brooch on her shoulder.

The importance of this contact in London between the Royal Family and the First Citizen of France cannot be overestimated. On his return to France the President told his people, "The British Royal Family gave me a delightful welcome, and the welcome of the British people was very enthusiastic.

"If there have been clouds over the friendship which unites our two peoples, I can assure you nothing of them remains."

This special quality of friendship between the Royal

Family and the President of France has remained, and is as firm and warm to-day, with M. René Coty as President, as it was in 1950. By reason of it co-operation between the two countries has been easier to achieve. It has become the symbol of the Entente Cordiale itself.

Princess Elizabeth was the guest of honour on March 22 at the banquet at the London Guildhall at which the Lord Mayor, Sir Frederick Rowland, launched his £2,000,000 National Thanksgiving Fund, to provide accommodation in London for overseas students, an expression of Britain's gratitude for the war-time food parcels. The Princess said, "No one in this historic Guildhall nor indeed in the whole country has better cause than I to speak with real depth of feeling for this project. . . .

"From all parts of the Commonwealth and from the United States of America great quantities of food, amounting to over two million pounds' weight, were sent to me as gifts on the occasion of my marriage, and I had the great happiness of distributing the remarkable number of over one hundred and forty thousand food parcels made up from them."

It had been Princess Elizabeth's own idea to distribute the food received in the form of food parcels to as many of Britain's needy widows as possible. After consultation with welfare organizations she decided that to qualify a widow must have children and be on supplementary relief.

She asked the Women's Voluntary Services to help to prepare the parcels, each of which was to contain twenty-two pounds of food—four kinds of canned meat, butter, shortening, sugar, milk-powder, egg-powder, fruit juices, chocolate, tea, soap, yeast, and several kinds of dried fruit. The Princess helped to pack some of the parcels herself when she visited the depot to see how the work was proceeding. And she ensured that every recipient should be told the name of an overseas friend who had sent food in order that thanks could be expressed.

After her Guildhall speech the Princess received many individual donations to the fund, but none which she appreciated more than one from Sydney, New South Wales. "I would like to add mine to the thanksgiving fund as I am one of the lucky ones privileged with an English trip next month to study my trade," the letter ran. "So that many less-privileged Aussies can come to study, please put my ten shillings in. Yours sincerely, Aussie. P.S. Happiness to the Prince."

On March 28 Princess Elizabeth flew to Malta to spend a few weeks with Prince Philip, First Lieutenant in the destroyer *Chequers*. There were to be few public engagements. Three weeks later the announcement that she was expecting her second child during the summer was made.

Just before leaving the island on May 9 she rented the Villa Guardamangia, a sign that she intended to make other extended visits.

The homeward trip was not without incident. A thunderstorm forced her plane to return to Nice after taking off on the last stage of the flight to London, and she spent a night at the Hôtel Negresco, facing the lovely Baie des Anges. The municipal authorities, with true Gallic consideration, dimmed the bright lights of the Promenade des Anglais that night so that, after the Princess retired early to bed, they would not disturb her rest. And when, next day, the Princess boarded her plane they filled her arms with flowers as she said good-bye.

Although she was officially temporarily retired from public affairs, Princess Elizabeth went with the other members of the Royal Family on May 27 to watch the Derby run. She was already revealing her interest in horses and their breeding and racing, but few in those days could suspect that this interest would soon become her most enthralling sport and hobby. As a child and young girl she had readily taken to the saddle, and during the War achieved considerable skill as a driver of a French pony-phaeton which was drawn by a pony called Hans. Yet her interest was not great in those days.

Later she showed her skill with horses by the speed with which she mastered the difficult art of riding side-saddle. It was perhaps at this period that she suddenly realized her very great interest in horses and set herself the task of mastering every phase of horsemanship. And all who know her declare that such a decision means that she will not rest until she has achieved her object. To-day she is an expert on horses of all kinds, and has an 'eye' for the horse that will make a flat racer, a steeplechaser, a show jumper, or an expert at dressage.

Thus no one was surprised when she also went with the Royal Family to Royal Ascot in June, although she remained in the shelter of the royal box almost throughout the hours of racing. But behind the scenes she was not allowing the approaching birth of her baby to affect her life any more than could be helped.

Prince Philip was promoted Lieutenant-Commander on July 16, and there was immediate talk of his getting his first command. But in the meantime he came home on special leave for the birth of his second child.

Princess Anne was born about noon on August 15. King George was at Balmoral shooting on the moors when the baby was born, for Princess Anne was late in arriving, and it was thought that it would be better for His Majesty to be enjoying his outdoor holiday in Scotland than to be waiting about in London for the birth. Prince Philip immediately telephoned the news to the King. The baby, who was born in Princess Elizabeth's own room at Clarence House, weighed six pounds.

That evening it was announced that Prince Philip was to take command of the frigate *Magpie*. He left London again for Malta on September 1 and joined his ship the next day.

Princess Elizabeth was undertaking public engagements again by the third week in October. Princess Anne was christened in the Music Room at Buckingham Palace on October 21, and there was a single-tier christening cake covered with white icing, topped by a silver cradle containing a baby dressed in ivory lace and edged with baskets of sugar flowers. Prince Charles was not prepared to be photographed after the ceremony, and the moment the lights were turned on he ran, sliding across the polished floor until he could take refuge behind a settee. From there he was gently but firmly lifted and carried back to the family group.

The Queen of the Netherlands and Prince Bernhard visited London on November 21 for a four-day State visit to King George and Queen Elizabeth, but Princess Elizabeth, although present at the State banquet on the first day, took less than the usual part in the various functions because Prince Philip, who had returned for a visit, was flying back to Malta to take over his ship, and she herself was following him on November 25.

This visit was in no way official. Princess Elizabeth was in the same position as the wife of any naval officer—she was joining her husband on his station. She sent her own car and forty large cases of clothes and personal effects ahead of her, and also a new polo pony for her husband,

and she determined to limit her public engagements to the minimum in order to enjoy the peace and the sunshine of her home in Malta to the utmost. But during her stay she did travel to Greece in the frigate *Surprise*—accompanied by Prince Philip in *Magpie*—to pay her respects to the King and Queen of Greece and call on Prince Philip's mother, Princess Andrew.

It was February 12, 1951, before Princess Elizabeth was back in England. Ahead of her lay a year that was many times more busy in terms of public engagements than 1950. Already more than a hundred major engagements were recorded in the Diary, and these did not include any in the long tour of Canada booked for October. At that time, although the Princess was concerned over her father's health, there was no immediate sign that there was anything serious in the King's indisposition. His Majesty, in fact, was hiding from his family the fact that he was feeling more and more the strain of public engagements and that he was experiencing trouble with his chest and breathing.

On March 19, the Princess was in Malta again, and from there, on April 11, she went to Rome and Florence with Prince Philip on a "private and informal" visit. It was a visit which was once more to bring about sharp protest from some Protestant organizations in Britain, for the Princess and her husband were received in private audience by the Pope. In fact, Princess Elizabeth was the sixth member of the British Royal Family to visit the Pontiff since Henry VIII had broken with the Vatican four centuries ago. King Edward VII was first to break with British tradition in this matter, as, indeed, he was with so many insular prejudices. The Duke of Windsor—as Prince of Wales—visited Pope Benedict XV in 1918, and King

George V and Queen Mary had an audience of Pius XI in 1923. Princess Margaret visited Pope Pius XII in 1949.

On one Sunday afternoon in Rome after church the Princess watched Prince Philip play polo for his ship's team. Private and unofficial though the visit was, the Princess and her husband managed to cram into their fortnight's stay a great number of engagements which had every appearance of being official. They were given great prominence in the Italian Press and evoked warm comments from observers. In fact, the greeting of orphaned fourteen-year-old Marcello Nicholich when the Royal holiday-makers visited the Boys' Town called Borgo Ragazzi Dom Bosco, on the outskirts of the city, was typical of the general comment. "Our gratitude is as great and splendid as anything in Rome," said Marcello, in specially burnished English. "We ask you to accept our gratitude as the gift of our hospitality."

But on May 24, exactly one month after Princess Elizabeth reached England again, the General Assembly of the Free Church of Scotland, besides demanding the recall of Britain's envoy to the Vatican, passed a resolution viewing "with deep concern the increasing tendency on the part of members of the Royal Family to be received in audience by the Pope." Dr Roy Whitehorn, one-time Moderator of the General Assembly of the Presbyterian Church of England, however, went on record with the view that "The Princess's visit to the Pope was an act of political courtesy—like the head of one State visiting the head of another."

Once again, however, Princess Elizabeth had had brought home to her the fact that her every action is watched by the world at large and that always there will be some section of the people who will criticize and complain. How much this need to be constantly on the alert for the unthinking movement or the incautious word is a strain on the members of the Royal Family it is difficult to say. Certainly King George VI was sensitive to public feeling in a way exceptional in kings, and unfair criticism of his daughter's actions in Rome undoubtedly caused him distress, more particularly at a time when his illness was becoming acute.

Only a week after the protests over the audience with the Pope and the complaints at Prince Philip's polo match on a Sunday of the Rome visit the King's doctors announced on June 1: "The King has been confined to his room for the past week with an attack of influenza.

"There is now a small area of catarrhal inflammation in the lung, but the constitutional disturbance is slight."

This was only a fortnight after the announcement of the names of those who would accompany the King and Queen on their tour of Australia.

Once again there were rumours of a cancellation of the trip and denials that such a move was contemplated. But behind the scenes Princess Elizabeth, busy with the preparations for her visit to Canada and the United States, was in fact already aware that if the King were again prevented by ill-health from making the trip she and Prince Philip would take his place, in order that there should not again be such widespread disappointment and consequent disruption of business in the Commonwealth.

5

Every Facet of Life

WHEN King George and Queen Elizabeth visited the Festival of Britain on the South Bank, London, on May 4, 1951, there was no hint that the King was ill. His Majesty moved from pavilion to pavilion with a brisk step and showed the greatest interest in everything that he saw. Yet he must already have been feeling the first onset of his illness, which was first described on May 25 as mild influenza.

It might have been thought that the almost casual wording of the bulletin at the time indicated that there was very little wrong with the King. However, on June 4 his doctors advised him to cancel all engagements. Those who were in His Majesty s closest confidence knew then that the King was really ill. Once again Princess Elizabeth and Prince Philip took on as many of the King's engagements as possible, but it was inevitable that a great number had to be cancelled.

King George was not able to take any public part in the welcome to King Haakon of Norway when he paid a State visit to London on June 5. At the banquet in the white-and-gold State Ballroom at Buckingham Palace, the same evening Princess Elizabeth read on the King's behalf a speech proposing the health of the King of Norway.

All Britain echoed King Haakon's words when he said, "We all hope His Majesty will soon recover after his illness, and I hope his illness will only be a short one."

On June 6 Princess Elizabeth opened the annual Antique Dealers' Fair and Exhibition at Grosvenor House, Park Lane, and took the opportunity of paying tribute to the great contribution Queen Mary had made to all that is beautiful. Here was an expression of of admiration for one of the leading authorities on antique furniture, china, and silver in the country. The Princess was aware that it was Queen Mary, more than anyone else, who turned Buckingham Palace from a vast storehouse of mixed treasures and useless junk into a home that was filled with some of the finest artistic creations in the world. It was Queen Mary who carefully sorted and tabulated all the items of furniture, china and silver, pictures and *objets d'art* that had been collected over more than a hundred years and gave them the place in the 600 rooms of the Palace that most of them still occupy to-day.

In opening the exhibition Princess Elizabeth declared that she herself was only a novice in the art of collecting, but that she owed all the knowledge she possessed to the advice of her grandmother with her faultless memory.

Princess Elizabeth took the place of the King at the ceremony of Trooping the Colour on Horse Guards Parade on June 7. She was setting a precedent, for this was the first occasion on which a princess had taken the traditional sovereign's parade.

That same evening King Haakon was entertained to dinner by the Queen at Buckingham Palace, and in the small party were Princess Elizabeth and Miss Margaret Truman, daughter of the President of the United States of America, Mr Harry S. Truman. Princess Elizabeth was, of course, already aware that there were plans for her to visit Canada and possibly the United States, although no official announcement had yet been made. She had talked over the matter of a visit to Canada the previous December with Mr Ross Macdonald, Speaker of the Canadian House of Commons, when he came to London, partly to obtain the views of the King on a possible trip. She had told Mr Macdonald that both she and Prince Philip would very much like to see Canada and its people. The Prime Minister of Canada, Mr Louis St Laurent, however, had been in correspondence with the King for some months, and the news of the King's illness had brought additional urgency to a decision. The King was anxious that there should be no postponement, and, although he himself knew that his own health could easily deteriorate seriously during the year, his advice was that the announcement should be made and that the Princess's tour should be carried through.

At the Buckingham Palace dinner the talk after the meal turned to North America, and Miss Truman, in describing Washington and life in the capital, sounded Princess Elizabeth on the possibility of her visiting the United States. The President's daughter took back to her father the news that the Princess and Prince Philip hoped that it would be possible for them to travel to Washington.

But before the announcement of the North American trip was made Princess Elizabeth had tours to carry out in the United Kingdom. On June 4 she visited Worcester; on the following day she was in Birmingham; on June 18 she travelled to Norwich for the Festival in the New Colman Art Gallery. On June 21 she went to Manchester for the ceremony of laying up of colours of the 3rd Battalion Grenadier Guards in the Cathedral.

At a dinner in London of the English-Speaking Union on July 3 General Dwight D. Eisenhower was the guest of honour, and it was here that Lord Salisbury announced that Princess Elizabeth had agreed to succeed him as President of the Union. King George had sent a telegram to Lord Salisbury which said, "I am glad to hear that my daughter, Princess Elizabeth, is to succeed you in your high office, and trust that in her presidency the Union will always prosper and continue the valuable work it is doing throughout the world."

It was appropriate that on the following day it was announced by Mr Louis St Laurent, the Canadian Prime Minister, in Ottawa, and from Clarence House that Princess Elizabeth and Prince Philip would visit Canada in October.

There had to be a decision on the projected tour of Australia and New Zealand by the King, which had been fixed for January 1952. On July 15 Mr Robert Menzies, Prime Minister of Australia, in association with Mr Sidney Holland, Prime Minister of New Zealand, wrote to Mr McKell, the Governor-General of Australia, regarding the advisability of the tour going through because of the possible injury to the King's health. "Having this feeling, both Mr Holland and I would like His Majesty to reconsider the matter without any commitment," the letter ran. "Would he like even the proposed programme modified? Would he like some postponement? Would he prefer that the tour be made by Her Majesty and/or Princess Elizabeth and/or Princess Margaret?

"In brief, we want to help and will fall in with any arrangement that may be proposed."

The King answered at once, and Mr McKell told the two Prime Ministers, "His Majesty is much touched by the kind feelings which prompted Mr Menzies and Mr Holland to send this message." But the King said that he still hoped to be able to make the trip.

Throughout the summer months the Princess and her husband were kept busy by a great variety of public engagements while at the same time making all necessary arrangements for the tour of North America. The announcement of the invitation to the United States and its acceptance had been made on July 13, and there was much to do to fit in the two visits. Princess Elizabeth had her wardrobe to select—a small selection in view of the short duration of the trip, but an important one in view of the great interest in British clothes on the other side of the Atlantic. Norman Hartnell and Hardy Amies were the dressmakers chosen, and there were many hurried consultations at Clarence House before the needlewomen could get to work.

Both Princess Elizabeth and Prince Philip had other important work to do before the great trip began. At every opportunity they studied the latest facts and figures relative to life and trade in Canada and the United States, the details of geography and climate, of race and religion. A great many books on the Dominion as well as Government publications arrived at Clarence House for their use. No fact was too trivial to be learned and digested, for they were anxious that they should be able to converse with intelligent knowledge with their hosts in both countries. And so it was that they continually surprised the people of Canada and the United States by their grasp of what life in North America was like and how the future was shaping.

The ordinary engagements of that summer were as varied in character as they could be. On July 14 Princess

Elizabeth attended the first concert of the National Federation of Jazz Organizations, held in the Royal Festival Hall, London, and three days later she received the Fellowship of the Royal College of Obstetricians and Gynæcologists and heard herself described as "the ideal of young womanhood and motherhood." On July 20 she visited Portsmouth, and on the following day went with her mother to see the King George VI Festival of Britain Stakes run at Ascot. Both the Queen and Princess Elizabeth had, in fact, registered their racing colours under Jockey Club rules in the previous March.

On July 23 with Prince Philip the Princess attended the open competition organized by the Foil Club and Amateur Fencing Association in Chelsea Town Hall, and on the following day presented her own cup at the International Horse Show. And so it went on almost every day with some public engagement that would identify the Princess and her husband with every facet of life in the country.

Towards the end of August rumours concerning the King's health began to reach London. On September 1 Dr Geoffrey Marshall, a famous specialist in chest ailments, and Dr George Cordiner, a radiologist, travelled north to Balmoral to examine the King. No announcement was made, and on the following morning His Majesty attended church at Crathie. It seemed that the doctors' examination had shown that the King's health was improving. On September 7, however, the King left Ballater for Euston, and next day he called on Dr Cordiner in his Wimpole Street consulting-rooms. After this visit His Majesty again left London to fly back to Dyce Airport, in Aberdeen, and Balmoral, and on September 9 he once more attended religious service at the little church of Crathie. Four more days passed, and in the evening of

September 13 King George received Dr A. Greig Anderson, his local doctor, and invested him with the insignia of Commander of the Victorian Order.

Two days later King George arrived back in London, and on September 18 he received the Prime Minister, Mr Clement Attlee, at Buckingham Palace. It appeared at the time that this meeting was the ordinary routine meeting of the Sovereign with his Prime Minister. In fact, the King then informed Mr Attlee that he was to be operated on within a few days. King George was in no doubt about the serious nature of his illness. In March 1949 he had learned that he was suffering from Buerger's disease, a serious condition of the arteries. And now he knew that he had bronchial carcinoma and that an operation, though essential, could not guarantee complete recovery.

The operation took place on September 23 at Buckingham Palace in the Buhl Room (which had been fitted up as an emergency operating theatre), and afterwards eight doctors issued a bulletin: "The King underwent an operation for lung resection this morning. Whilst anxiety must remain for some days His Majesty's immediate post-operative condition is satisfactory."

On September 27 the King set up a Council of State, with the Queen, Princess Elizabeth, Princess Margaret, the Duke of Gloucester, and the Princess Royal as its members. That Council was to act until December 10.

Despite his determination to carry out the visit to Australia and New Zealand the King had to announce on October 9 that he would not be able to make the trip and that Princess Elizabeth and Prince Philip would go in his stead. The announcement ran:

"On his doctor's advice the King has now regretfully decided that, since his projected tour would follow so soon after his severe operation, he will be unable to visit Australia and New Zealand next year.

"As suggested jointly by Mr Menzies and Mr Holland last June, His Majesty has asked the Princess Elizabeth and the Duke of Edinburgh to carry out this part of the tour for him, which their Royal Highnesses will very gladly do."

It had been planned that the King and the Queen would sail from Southampton on January 22 in the Shaw Savill liner *Gothic* and that their route would be via Gibraltar, Malta, Port Said, Suez, Aden, Colombo, and the Cocos Islands. It was intended that they should reach Fremantle on March 1 and visit every State, but not the Capital Territory or Northern Territory. Their New Zealand tour was to begin at Wellington on May 6 and end at Auckland on June 7.

That programme now became the basis of the planning for Princess Elizabeth and Prince Philip, but in the discussions that began immediately and were continued even while they were in Canada several alternatives were put forward.

On the day of their departure from London Airport for the Atlantic crossing by the B.O.A.C. aircraft *Canopus* Princess Elizabeth and the Prince went to see the King in his sickroom, and he told them laughingly of how one of his doctors had crashed his car at the very gates of the Palace. He seemed much improved in health and taking an interest in what was going on around him.

Princess Elizabeth and Prince Philip had said good-bye to their children in the early evening of October 7, but before they set out for London Airport for the take-off at 11.30 P.M. they tiptoed into the nursery to take a last look at the sleeping Prince and Princess. A little over ten hours later Princess Elizabeth and Prince Philip were in Canada.

The tour of Canada was a triumph from the start. A little shy, even perhaps a little uncertain at the outset, for it was her first big overseas tour, Princess Elizabeth soon won the hearts of all Canadians, and Prince Philip was immediately popular because of his so obvious solicitude for his wife at all times and because of his ready wit. French-Canadians were delighted with the Princess's command of the French language, and all were pleased with the easy banter of the Duke and his skill as an after-dinner speaker.

The tour was arduous and the weather sometimes trying, but both the Princess and her husband came up smiling always. It was admitted that the Princess had sometimes been tired, but certainly she had never been bored. From time to time during the tour she telephoned London—on the first occasion from the train carrying them from Montreal to Quebec on the first day of the visit—so that she could be assured that her father was making progress. In fact, five calls were made to Buckingham Palace during the month-long journey.

Princess Elizabeth was surprised and delighted by the warmth of the Canadian welcome. And when, in Victoria, British Columbia, she had her hair shampooed and waved she confided in Miss Doris Stenmark, her hairdresser, that, although she had prepared herself for the vastness of the country before setting out from Britain, she had never realized how enormous it really was.

The memories built up during the trip were limitless. The Princess met old friends whom she had not expected to see—Mrs T. R. Bennetts, of Salmon Arm, British Columbia, who had lived near Glamis Castle and had been a childhood playmate of the Queen, and Mr Stanley Woodeson, who was once a policeman at Sandringham.

The Duke, when he visited H.M.C.S. *Discovery* at Vancouver, met several friends of the War days, including Captain Donald Smith, under whom he had served in the troop-carrying *Empress of Asia*, and Commodore Maurice Mayall, who had commanded the *Empress of Russia*. Commodore Mayall recalled how the Prince had had to help shovel coal in the stokehold of the ship in 1941 and had developed a good crop of blisters. And Captain Smith announced afterwards that the Prince had not lost his skill as a mimic. "He can sit in a cabin and imitate two British sailors having a chat below decks, and unless you saw him you would never believe the two voices were coming from the same man," he said.

Princess Elizabeth, despite the many lovely dresses she took with her, several times wore a dress or a coat on a second and sometimes third occasion at an official function.

In their brief visit to the United States the royal couple gained an equal popularity. Princess Elizabeth, called "My dear" by the fatherly President Truman and referred to as "the Fairy Princess," was voted "a symbol of British lustre, dignity, and strength."

President Truman, indeed, showed his delight at having had the opportunity of entertaining the royal couple, and he did not hide his belief that their visit would do incalculable good to the cause of Anglo-American understanding. Throughout the country, although the visit was so short, and confined as it was to the immediate surroundings of the capital, there was a greater realization of the place of the sovereign in the Commonwealth by the time the Princess and her husband flew away again, and this was reflected in the newspaper comments when King George died. Then Princess Elizabeth became simply "The Queen" in newspapers published in the most rabidly 'isolationist' areas of the United States.

Home again on November 17 for a traditional welcome from the City of London at the Guildhall, Princess Elizabeth heard Mr Winston Churchill say, "Madam, when you and your husband left us in days of deep anxiety for the safety of the King every one understood and realized the emotions, on leaving your father's side at so critical a moment, which you must have experienced, but it was his wish that you should fulfil your mission to the great Dominion which rejoices in its partnership in the British Commonwealth and Empire."

And Sir Leslie Boyce, the Lord Mayor, recalled the dedication to service made by Princess Elizabeth in Cape Town in 1947. "Through all the strenuous days just accomplished," he said, "in every word and action, how utterly has Her Royal Highness fulfilled the promises of that noble resolution."

Princess Elizabeth was still unaware of the almost desperate nature of her father's illness. The King was all the time assuring those close to him that he was better, so that on December 10 the Council of State was revoked and His Majesty resumed his conduct of State affairs.

The Princess and Prince Philip continued with their public engagements. Princess Elizabeth was admitted an honorary Fellow of the Royal College of Surgeons at Lincoln's Inn Fields, London, on December 5. "The astonishing development of surgery during the fifty-one years since the college received its first charter, and the seeming miracles it performs to-day, are things in which laymen and experts alike rejoice. My own family, like so many others, has the best reason in the world to be glad of it," she said then.

In truth, the operation on the King had been a near-miracle. His Majesty saw in the readiness with which his medical advisers acceded to his requests to be allowed to resume his work the acceptance of the fact that he had at most a few years to live.

It was the King who insisted that he should be allowed to make his customary Christmas Day broadcast to the world, and all the world sat shocked while listening to the voice of a dying man. The hoarse voice, the audible battling for breath, the obvious courage, though they shocked millions and brought the King waves of sympathy, also brought unbelievable admiration of His Majesty.

Round him at Sandringham the King had that Christmas the most complete gathering of members of the Royal Family since the War. That also was a sign of the serious nature of the King's condition.

Yet His Majesty insisted on being at London Airport on January 31, 1952, when Princess Elizabeth and Prince Philip set out on their tour of the Commonwealth by way of Nairobi, Kenya. The picture of the King, hatless in the cold wind, his face drawn and haggard, was flashed round the world. Millions were saddened but few were surprised at the news which came only a week later, on February 6, that King George VI had died in his sleep at his home at Sandringham.

6

Queen at Twenty-five

PRINCESS ELIZABETH was resting in the sitting-room of Sagana Lodge at Nyeri, Kenya, on February 6, 1952, when the telephone rang in another room. Lieutenant-Commander Parker, Prince Philip's Private Secretary, answered it. A voice at the other end of the line said, "Mike, this is Martin. Granville Roberts, of the *East African Standard*, has received a report of the death of the King. I think I had better get the news confirmed officially."

It was Lieutenant-Colonel Martin Charteris, Princess Elizabeth's Private Secretary, speaking. He had been summoned to the telephone booth at the Outspan Hotel, seventeen miles from Nyeri.

Granville Roberts had been trying to get through to Sagana Lodge, but had been unable to make contact, and it was not until Colonel Charteris arrived at the telephone that the connexion was made.

It was 2.15 P.M. Princess Elizabeth and Prince Philip had not long returned to the royal lodge after an exciting night in Treetops, the hotel in a giant fig-tree overlooking a water-hole in the Aberdare Forest game reserve. They had walked along forest paths for more than half a mile after leaving their car, and, with a white hunter, rifle ready, at their head and Prince Philip with elephant gun in his hand bringing up the rear, they came at last to the clearing beside Treetops. And there, not more than fifteen yards away, stood a trumpeting elephant, with ten others standing silent at the water-hole. While Prince Philip and the white hunter stood guard Princess Elizabeth and the rest of the party climbed the ladder into the famous hotel in the tree.

There, by the artificial moonlight provided by the hotel, they watched the animals come out of the forest to drink —elephants, waterbuck, baboons, more elephants with calves, and rhinoceros and their calves.

Neither of the royal travellers went to bed that night, but rested instead in chairs until the hunters informed them that there were new and interesting sights to be seen down below in the clearing. And so it was probably at some moment when she was taking pictures of African wild life with her cine-camera that Princess Elizabeth, without knowing it, became Queen.

Mr Sherbrooke Walker, the owner of Treetops, said to the Princess next morning before she left for Sagana Lodge, "If you have the same courage, Ma'am, in facing whatever the future sends you as you have in facing an elephant at ten yards, we are going to be very fortunate."

On the way back to Sagana Lodge the Princess had been happy and excited. She had talked with the Duke of the possibility that her father, when his health was restored, might come to the lodge—a wedding present to the Princess from the Government and people of Kenya—for his convalescence, and also to experience the thrills of a night at Treetops. The royal travellers were tired and grimy, for Princess Elizabeth, in order to conserve the water that has to be carried in cans on the heads of porters to Treetops, had had only the most perfunctory wash, and

Prince Philip had not shaved. But they were both relaxed and happy.

At 2.45 P.M. Lieutenant-Colonel Charteris, having previously confirmed the news of His Majesty's death, arrived at Sagana Lodge. Prince Philip had been told the news by Lieutenant-Commander Parker, and Princess Elizabeth had in turn been told by her husband.

Princess Elizabeth broke down and wept for some minutes. Here was confirmation of her worst fears, fears which she had been putting away from her in face of the King's indomitable fight for recovery and his optimism. For a few moments there was no thought of anything but her grief.

Then the training of a lifetime asserted itself. Queen Elizabeth II, face white and tear-stained, turned to her husband and began to plan the immediate future. They must leave for home as soon as a plane could be provided. There must be messages to her mother and Queen Mary, to the Prime Minister in London, to the Prime Ministers of Australia, New Zealand, and Ceylon, and to the Government of Kenya. The liner *Gothic*, waiting at Mombasa to take them on to Ceylon, must be warned. For the next hour or so Colonel Charteris and Commander Parker were hurrying in and out of the sitting-room with cable forms and scribbled telephone messages. The Queen was quite composed, and only the bleakness of her eyes showed the full extent of her grief.

Her Majesty gave orders to her personal maid, Miss "Bobo" Macdonald, to pack as soon as it was confirmed that the homeward flight could be made at once. Prince Philip's valet set to work to pack his master's clothes.

As soon as all these details had been seen to the Queen sat down in the sitting-room and began to autograph photographs of herself. And before the royal couple set out for Nanyuki to board the plane the Queen had all the staff of the royal lodge summoned to her so that she could give each a signed photograph, a shake of the hand, and a word of thanks. The Somalis and Goans stood in the drive to wave the royal car away.

At the airport lines of Africans stood waiting, heads bowed and murmuring their sorrow. The Queen shook hands with the airport officials, the crew of the plane, and then, in beige dress and white hat, walked up the gangway to the East African Airways plane which was to take them to Entebbe, in Uganda.

In Britain and all over the Commonwealth the machinery of the royal accession was in motion. This was the first occasion in British history that a sovereign had acceded while overseas in the Commonwealth, although King George I was in Hanover when Queen Anne died in 1714. It was noted that Queen Elizabeth II was ascending the throne at the same age—twenty-five—as the first Queen Elizabeth and that for the first time in history Britain and the Commonwealth had three living Queens but no King.

The people talked of that last farewell of the King and his daughter only a week before—how King George and the Queen and Princess Margaret had driven from Buckingham Palace to London Airport to see the Argonaut plane which was to carry the royal couple to Nairobi set off. A great crowd had given all the Royal Family a tremendous reception, but the sight of the King had brought fear to many hearts. King George had looked very ill as he strode across the tarmac to the plane and went aboard for the last farewells with his daughter and her husband. Still, there had been vigour in the wave he gave them as the aircraft began to taxi out for the take-off, even if his face looked old and very grey.

The royal party had gone up on to the roof of the airport lounge to watch the plane take off. And the King, waving again even though his arm became slower and slower, stood motionless, watching until the Argonaut was only a speck in the distant sky. The Queen, by his side, had had to touch his arm to remind him that it was time to go. Was the King at that moment convinced that he would never see his daughter again?

They had always been so close to each other, with a perfect understanding of each other's thoughts and actions. Did the King at that moment remember his words at the grave of Cecil Rhodes in the Matopo Hills in 1947, "Poor Elizabeth. . . . She will be lonely all her life." At that time Mr P. B. Fletcher, the Southern Rhodesian Minister for Native Affairs, had been with the King and had asked if he should accompany the Princess. "I would like that," answered King George. As Mr Fletcher approached Princess Elizabeth had said, without turning her head, "Mr Fletcher, what a wonderful shrine you have here." The Minister asked how she had known it was he who had approached, and the Princess replied, "I saw you with the King, and I knew he would send you down to me."

All this was being remembered and talked about as the new Queen flew through the tropical night towards her destiny. On February 8 she made her Accession Declaration to members of the Privy Council at a meeting at St James's Palace, subscribed the oath relating to the security of the Church of Scotland, and approved several Orders-in-Council. "At this time of deep sorrow it is a profound consolation to me to be assured of the sympathy which you and all my people feel towards me, to my mother and my sister, and to the other members of my family. My father was our revered and beloved head, as he was of the wider family of his subjects; the grief which his loss brings is shared among us all.

"My heart is too full for me to say more to you to-day than that I shall always work, as my father did throughout his reign, to uphold constitutional government and to advance the happiness and prosperity of my peoples. . . .

'I pray that God will help me to discharge worthily this heavy task that has been laid upon me so early in my life."

The public proclamation of the accession of the Queen was made immediately afterwards outside St James's Palace, at Charing Cross and Temple Bar, from the steps of the Royal Exchange, at the Tower of London, and from the balcony of the Middlesex Guildhall. The proclamation was read in Scotland, in Wales, and in Northern Ireland, in the cities of England, and in the Commonwealth countries overseas:

"That the High and Mighty Princess Elizabeth Alexandra Mary is now, by the death of our late Sovereign of happy memory, become Queen Elizabeth II, by the Grace of God, Queen of this Realm, and of Her other Realms and Territories, Head of the Commonwealth, Defender of the Faith, to whom all Her Lieges do acknowledge all Faith and constant Obedience, with hearty and humble Affection, beseeching God, by Whom Kings and Queens do reign, to bless the Royal Princess, Elizabeth II, with long and happy years to reign over us. God Save the Queen."

Queen Elizabeth saw herself being proclaimed Queen by watching the television set in her drawing-room at Clarence House, and thus again made history by being the first sovereign to see as well as hear the heralds make their proclamation.

In the afternoon the Queen, with Prince Philip, left London for Sandringham, where her mother and Princess Margaret were still in residence, and where the body of the King still lay in the bedroom where he had died. But the Queen did not enter her father's room, despite the widely held belief that she did so.

At five in the afternoon Her Majesty watched her father's coffin carried into Sandringham Church, where it was to lie until the following Monday. On Sunday Prince Charles and Princess Anne, who had been at Sandringham with the Queen Mother while their parents were in Africa, left by car for Clarence House.

At 10.30 on Monday, February 11, a service was held in Sandringham Church, and the King's coffin was then drawn to Wolferton Station on a gun carriage while all the estate workers watched bareheaded. From King's Cross Station the coffin was taken to Westminster Hall, where a short service attended by the Queen, the Queen Mother, Queen Mary, and Princess Margaret was held at 4.15 P.M.

The royal visitors from overseas were now arriving in London for the funeral. First to arrive at Buckingham Palace was the King of Norway, and he was followed by the King and Queen of Sweden, the King of the Hellenes, the Queen and Prince of the Netherlands.

There was a private dinner party at Buckingham Palace on February 13 at which the King of the Hellenes and Prince Ernst Augustus of Hanover were the principal guests. Before that took place the Duke of Windsor was entertained to tea by the Queen, Prince Philip, and the Queen Mother.

A deputation had come that morning from the House of Commons to present an address to the Queen on her accession. Her Majesty knew most of the Members, but there were some she had not met before. Mr Winston Churchill brought twenty-two M.P.'s to the Bow Room, which looks out on to the terrace of Buckingham Palace, at 11 A.M. on February 13. Mr Attlee, leader of the Opposition, was there, and there were ten Ministers among the party. The Prime Minister introduced each Member in turn to the Queen and Prince Philip. Among the Labour M.P.'s was Mr Aneurin Bevan.

Already the endless stream of official business was sweeping over the new Queen. On February 14, while Prince Philip was at London Airport at 10.45 to welcome the President of France, the Queen was dealing with correspondence which had swelled to several thousand letters a day—most of them letters of condolence from people both known and unknown in all parts of the world. At noon the Queen received the Right Hon. S. G. Holland, Prime Minister of New Zealand. At 1.30 P.M. she saw the Crown Prince of Norway and Princess Astrid, and immediately afterwards gave lunch to the King and Queen of Sweden, the Queen of the Netherlands and Prince Bernhard. Lord and Lady Mountbatten were also among the guests.

At 3 P.M. Queen Elizabeth received the High Commissioners of Commonwealth countries, Ministers, Ambassadors, and Foreign Ministers, and the representatives of Ireland. At 3.15 P.M. she received the representatives of foreign heads of State and the heads of overseas missions in London and other representatives who had come to London for the King's funeral.

At 6.30 the Queen received the President of the French

Republic and at 6.45 the President of the Turkish Republic. A quarter of an hour later she was greeting the President of the Præsidium of Yugoslavia, and at 7.30 she set out with Prince Philip and Princess Margaret for Westminster Hall, where the King's body was lying in state.

That was the last official engagement of a crowded day. But in the week ahead there were many days as crowded as this. Her first audience for the Prime Minister had been on February 12 at Clarence House, when Mr Winston Churchill, who had succeeded Mr Attlee in October 1951, offered his personal condolences and his assurances of unwavering support. The association of Mr Winston Churchill with the Queen, in which there was no question of political belief, had always been something more than that of Prime Minister and Sovereign by reason of the fact that Mr Churchill was a Minister of the Crown for a great part of the life of the Queen until her accession. He served in office or in Parliament under four sovereigns, and therefore had closer contact with the Palace than any other living statesman. Government business apart, the Queen regarded Sir Winston as a close personal friend whose advice on a wide variety of subjects could be sought and acted on. Thus, business matters disposed of, they could always converse with spirit on such widely separated subjects as art and horse racing—matters very close to both their hearts.

The extraordinary scenes at the Lying-in-State, when queues of people from all walks of life and from many countries filed slowly through Westminster Hall from early morning until two o'clock the next morning, were repeated at the funeral on February 15. All London crowded into the streets to pay the last respects to a King who had already passed into history as George the Good.

Here was pageantry, martial splendour, and simplicity linked by sombre but majestic sound—the slow, sad funeral music of the bands as they paced the long procession through the streets to Paddington Station mingled with the clatter of horses' hooves, the measured tread of feet in step, and the murmurings of the vast crowd that were like the washing of a great tide against an endless shore.

On the coffin shrouded in the Royal Standard the glittering Crown and the Orb and Sceptre and the insignia of the Order of the Garter marked the passing of a King. But in the crowds who watched the thoughts were only of the passing of a friend. There were 305,806 people who paid homage to the King in Westminster Hall, and now millions added their last tribute.

At Windsor the coffin was lowered into the royal vaults under St George's Chapel in the Castle, and the Queen, a lonely figure heavily veiled, sprinkled earth upon it from a gilded bowl.

The Queen's face was white under the veil, and her eyes showed her grief, but in her face also there was a serenity and a purpose that said as plainly as words that no personal sadness would alter her resolution to carry on the office of kingship where her father had left off, and without respite.

After the funeral Queen Elizabeth lost no time in getting to know every aspect of Government life in the country and overseas. There were meetings—on February 19 the last of the overseas mourners had returned to their homes —with Mr Dean Acheson, M. Robert Schuman, and Dr Adenauer, in London to discuss the future status of Germany. On each occasion Mr Anthony Eden, the Foreign Secretary, was present. The Queen showed at these meetings a remarkable insight into the problems that faced the politicians in arriving at a situation which would satisfy French fears for the future and German ideas of sovereignty.

On February 28 the Queen invited Field-Marshal Lord Alexander and Lady Alexander to lunch at Clarence House at the end of Lord Alexander's term of office as Governor-General of Canada. They were able to talk over the Queen's trip to the Dominion and the memories it had left in Canadian minds. Lord Alexander was able to give the Queen the latest news from the Dominion, including the development of public thought that more and more placed the Queen in the personal rôle of Queen of Canada, which was expressed in suggestions that she should visit the Dominion more frequently and maintain a permanent establishment there where she could spend long periods of full-time residence.

Apart from the Lord Chancellor, on February 28, and the Prime Minister, who had reported weekly from February 12, Lord Ismay, Secretary of State for Commonwealth Relations, was the first of her Ministers whom the Queen received in private audience. He went to Clarence House on March 5. His visit signified the eagerness with which the Queen was approaching the task of providing closer and closer links between the various member nations of the Commonwealth.

The Chancellor of the Exchequer, Mr R. A. Butler, was received on March 10, the Lord Privy Seal, the Marquis of Salisbury, on the following day, and Mr Anthony Eden, the Foreign Secretary, on March 18. On March 19 Mr H. F. C. Crookshank, Minister of Health, saw Her Majesty, and Sir Walter Monckton, Minister of Labour, had an audience at Clarence House on March 28. It was the turn of Miss Florence Horsbrugh, Minister of Education, on April 3, and of Mr Duncan Sandys, Minister of Supply, on the following day. Lord De La Warr, the Postmaster-General, went to Clarence House on April 8, and Mr Peter Thorneycroft, President of the Board of Trade, on April 9. Mr Gwilym Lloyd-George, Minister of Food, had his audience on May 8. In the same period the Queen also received seven High Commissioners and Governors of the Commonwealth, and met all the heads of missions of the Diplomatic Corps.

A meeting of great importance took place on May 15, when the Queen received General of the Army Dwight D. Eisenhower and Mrs Eisenhower and entertained them to luncheon afterwards. General Eisenhower was returning to America after relinquishing command of the N.A.T.O. forces. He was going back to the United States to become a contender for candidature in the United States presidential elections.

There could have been no certainty then that General Eisenhower would become President nor that he would control the policies of the United States for two terms of office, but the possibility that the General might secure nomination by his political party was discussed, and all that success at the polls would mean.

General Eisenhower and the Queen were old friends of war-time days. In 1946 he had stayed with the Royal Family at Balmoral, and it is reported that there Princess Elizabeth had taught him how to dance an eightsome reel.

In May 1952 there was a possibility that President Truman might run for President again. The Queen had developed a firm friendship with the kindly man from Missouri, and now she had renewed a friendship with a leading rival on the other side of the political fence. Without in any way desiring to enter into American politics,

"Above all we must keep alive that courageous spirit of adventure that is the finest quality of youth," the Queen said in 1952 in her first Christmas broadcast. Her Majesty sat in the same chair and at the same desk in the study from which all previous royal Christmas broadcasts had been made by her father and grandfather.

80

The Queen is crowned. The Coronation is over. Her Majesty, with sceptre and rod with the dove in her hands, waits to come down from her throne.

The Queen is an expert on horses of all kinds—flat racers, steeplechasers, show jumpers. And she has an encyclopædic knowledge of the thoroughbreds of the Stud Book. At the races she finds she can get the maximum of relaxation from the affairs of State. Here she is seen with Queen Elizabeth the Queen Mother at Epsom for the Derby of 1957.

81

Alison, Marigold, and Mary Peddie receive from the Queen a special prize in the children's riding class at the Royal Windsor Show held at Windsor in July 1952. The show had been postponed owing to the death of King George VI and Her Majesty's accession.

the Queen, believing that it was of the utmost importance that all in authority in Britain should understand the American point of view, therefore welcomed this opportunity of hearing at first hand from some one who was to be soon in the middle of an election fight.

That night General and Mrs Eisenhower dined at 10 Downing Street with Mr and Mrs Churchill. In the afternoon General Eisenhower had called on Queen Mary at Marlborough House.

The Queen entertained to tea on May 16 the Regent of Iraq, who had come to London with Iraq's Prime Minister, Nuri es Said, to discuss Middle East problems, particularly Britain's relations with Egypt. Here was an opportunity for learning about a new area of the world which the Queen was glad to have, apart from helping to strengthen the close ties between Iraq and Britain.

Between January and the end of May the Queen carried out a great number of public engagements, and already the medical world was becoming alarmed at the possibility that she might overtax her strength in attempting to carry out the full responsibilities of her official position while at the same time looking after her children and running the domestic side of her home.

"As mother of a young family and mistress of a home she has a life of her own whose happy fulfilment her subjects would place first," declared *The Lancet*.

"Already thus accepted as parent and wife, she now becomes permanent head of the Governments of her several realms, and must gradually acquire the knowledge and experience of their affairs which is needed even by the most constitutional of monarchs, together with the range of interests appropriate to the most representative of citizens. Finally, as Sovereign, she must discharge the ceremonial functions of Royalty: it is here especially that precautions are required.

"The grace and gaiety shown by Princess Elizabeth on her travels have made many forget how great can be the strain of ceremonial engagements, particularly when in series.

"Of late the medical profession has become more and more aware of the physical price paid by those subjected to too frequent or continuous strain nowadays imposed on Royalty.

"As doctors, therefore, we should have a special reason to welcome an assurance that, by deliberate decisions taken in advance, Her Majesty's health and vitality will be protected from Her Majesty's hereditary sense of duty."

The Queen carried out 140 engagements in the five months to June 1. In the next seven months she carried out 308—an increase of more than 50 per cent.

7

Beyond the Safeties

For the Queen 1952 was a year of apprenticeship and preparation. There was so much to learn about her difficult job, so much to decide and prepare for. On April 28 she had named June 2, 1953, for her Coronation, and at the same time she appointed a Coronation Commission of thirty-six representatives from Britain, Canada, Australia, New Zealand, South Africa, Pakistan, and Ceylon to plan the great occasion. Prince Philip was appointed chairman of the Commission, with the Earl Marshal, the Duke of Norfolk, as his deputy.

The Commission appointed on May 5 a twenty-man Committee to handle the day-by-day business and to report back to the full Commission. This Committee met at St James's Palace for the first time on May 19 under the chairmanship of the Duke of Norfolk, and the first plans of the Coronation route and of the ceremony itself in Westminster Abbey were produced for the Queen. It was then decided that the work of issuing invitations, working out the strict timetable of the day, and of planning receptions should be the responsibility of an even smaller executive committee presided over by the Duke of Norfolk.

The Queen and Prince Philip moved into their new apartments at Buckingham Palace on May 5, and the Royal Standard flew over the Palace for the first time since the previous reign. They occupied the Belgian Suite on the ground floor—so called because it had always been used by Leopold I, the King of the Belgians, when he visited his niece, Queen Victoria. The suite had been intended for King George IV, the idea being to save him the fatigue of climbing stairs to bed, but that sovereign died before the place was finished. William IV and Queen Adelaide chose rooms on the first floor, which in turn they never occupied, but which became the suite of Queen Victoria, and which the Sovereign has usually occupied ever since. Now these rooms, which she had occupied since 1937, were to remain for the time being as the suite of Queen Elizabeth the Queen Mother. Princess Margaret's suite was at the opposite end of the Palace over the Visitors' Entrance. Prince Charles and Princess Anne had their own small nursery suite on the second floor.

At a Coronation Council held at Buckingham Palace on June 6 the Queen signed a Proclamation appointing June 2, 1953, as the date of the Coronation and named forty-two Privy Councillors to form the Court of Claims which would examine the standing of all who claimed the right to perform special services for the Queen at the ceremony. In the Court of Claims, an ancient court dating from 1377, when it was set up before the Coronation of Richard II, were Prince Philip, the Duke of Gloucester, Mr Churchill, the Archbishop of Canterbury, the Duke of Norfolk, the Duke of Hamilton (Lord Steward), the Duke of Beaufort (Master of the Horse), and Mr Clement Attlee (leader of the Opposition).

On the following morning the Proclamation procession set out—the Heralds and Pursuivants, colourful in their Elizabethan tabards. The first reading was from the balcony of Friary Court, St James's Palace, by Sir George

Trooping the Colour, 1953—one of the great events of the London Season. Here the Queen, in Coronation Year, crosses Horse Guards Parade before taking the salute.

By courtesy of the Air Ministry

Bellew, Garter King of Arms; the second at King Charles's Statue, Charing Cross, by Mr Archibald Russell, the Lancaster Herald; the third, after entry into the City of London had been acceded by the Lord Mayor, Sir Leslie Boyce, at the corner of Chancery Lane and Fleet Street, by Sir Gerald Wollaston, Norroy and Ulster King of Arms; and the fourth and last reading was from the steps of the Royal Exchange by Sir Arthur Cochrane, Clarenceux King of Arms.

But not all the Queen's time could be taken up by purely Coronation business. Her Majesty continued to handle the vast mass of correspondence which flowed increasingly into the Palace from the self-governing countries of the Commonwealth. On June 10 the Queen received the Sultan of Brunei at the Palace. His Highness had brought from his home in Borneo two silver rose-bowls for the Queen, a silver inkstand for Prince Philip, silver candlesticks for the Queen Mother, and gold sarongs woven by his wife for Princess Margaret and Queen Mary.

At this meeting the proposal for a visit to Brunei later in the year was discussed. This was to form part of a tour of Malaya and Borneo by the Duchess of Kent and her son the young Duke of Kent, and the Queen was delighted to be able to talk at first hand with some one who would be a host to the royal travellers.

There were also many requests for portrait sittings to satisfy the great desire of corporations and public bodies for a portrait of the Queen. Her Majesty had to examine very carefully all the requests. Miss Dorothy Wilding took the first official photographs in April, and the Queen and Prince Philip spent a long time deciding which were the best. These formed the portraits for use on the new stamps.

The Queen granted portrait sittings to Mr Douglas

Chandor, the famous American portrait-painter, to Mr Cecil Thomas, Mr G. H. Paulin, to Mr Carter Preston, Mr Gilbert Ledward, Miss Lindsay Williams, Miss Stella Marks, the Australian, and to Mr Edward Halliday. Here was an additional burden of work, for long hours of sitting for a portrait can be as tiring as any more obviously strenuous job. It is a strain that Her Majesty has recently most reluctantly had to reduce by cutting down the number of portraits for which she will grant sittings.

Between June 25 and June 30 the Queen was in Scotland in residence in the Palace of Holyroodhouse, Edinburgh. During her stay in the Scottish capital she revealed once more her attachment to tradition when she took part in the ancient ceremony of *servitium lavacri*, which had previously been performed only on two occasions—in 1822 and 1927—although its origin dates back more than four hundred years. Her Majesty had herself suggested that the ceremony should be included in her programme.

The service commemorates an occasion when James V of Scotland was attacked by robbers near Cramond, outside Edinburgh, and was rescued by Jock Houison, a farm servant, who did not know the identity of the rescued man. The King invited Jock to the Palace of Holyroodhouse, where James V revealed his identity and gave the farm-hand the lands of Braehead, for which Houison and his descendants were to provide a silver basin and ewer ready for any occasion on which a reigning monarch might pass their way.

Mr John D. Houison-Crauford, the holder of the tenure of Braehead, Cramond Bridge, presented the silver basin filled with rose-water, into which the Queen dipped her fingers.

Following the Scottish visit, the Queen travelled on July 1 to Devon for the Royal Agricultural Society Show at Newton Abbot, opening on the following day, and on July 3 she visited the farms on manors owned by the Duchy of Cornwall in Dorset and Wiltshire.

On July 16 the Queen held an evening presentation party for members of the Diplomatic Corps at the Court of St James's. This was the first great reception of her reign, and Her Majesty went back to the full ceremonial for the occasion. Gone, for one evening at least, was the austerity of the immediate post-War years. The Queen, in wonderful gown and diamond tiara, with her Court, moved through the crowded State apartments, in which more than a thousand guests were gathered. The American Embassy party alone was so large that an entire State room was given over to its members.

The members of the Honorable Corps of Gentlemen-at-Arms, in their scarlet coats with velvet facings and gold lace, ornamental halberds, and white gloves and their white-plumed, gilded helmets, stood guard in the various rooms.

At 9.30 the doors of the Picture Gallery were thrown open, and Lord Clarendon, the Lord Chamberlain, his white wand of office in his hand, preceded the Queen and Prince Philip and the other members of the Royal Family—the Duke and Duchess of Gloucester, the Princess Royal, the Duchess of Kent, Princess Alice Countess of Athlone and the Earl of Athlone. The long lines of women fell into deep curtsies as the Queen passed them, the men bowed their heads. Her Majesty paused briefly to chat to some of her guests and then passed on to the State Ballroom, where, under the magnificent canopy that had been made for her grandfather's Coronation Durbar in Delhi in 1911, she waited to meet all her guests.

For almost three hours the Queen remained with them. While they, in turn, had refreshments she continued to greet individual guests—to talk to Ambassadors and their senior staff members—the United States, French, and Soviet Ambassadors prominent among them. And in her conversations she revealed how well she had informed herself on events in other countries.

In the background Mr Winston Churchill stood, hardly taking his eyes off his Sovereign. In them was an obvious pride in her wonderful bearing and spirit. Her Majesty revealed again her amazing memory for faces and for facts. Time and again she greeted guests whom she had met only once before with their names, and was able to discuss with them incidents of their daily lives which revealed the close personal interest Her Majesty always takes in any who are to be her guests. The burden of extra work and study that the Queen always shoulders in order to put her guests at ease and give them immediate topics of conversation is both enormous and a continued source of surprise and alarm to her advisers.

The Queen stayed at Arundel Castle as the guest of the Duke of Norfolk between July 29 and August 1, and each day attended the racing at Goodwood. In 1952 Her Majesty was racing her fourteen horses in the name of the Duke of Norfolk. She had five at the Beckhampton, Wiltshire, stables of Mr Noel Murless, all of them leased by her father from the National Stud, and nine with Captain Cecil Boyd-Rochfort at Freemason's Lodge, Newmarket. These last nine included Aureole, much fancied by some for the Coronation Derby on account of his breeding by Hyperion out of Angelola.

Her Majesty's visit to Goodwood was the first made by a sovereign since the reign of George V. On that occasion the King stayed at Goodwood House, but the Royal suite had now been turned into a club for estate workers.

Prince Philip was in Helsinki for the Olympic Games from July 26 until August 3, but on August 4 he flew in the de Havilland Comet aircraft from the Finnish capital to Oslo, and from there straight to London. He had come home for Cowes Week, when he raced *Bluebottle*, the Dragon-class yacht given to the Queen and Prince Philip as a wedding gift.

The Queen, although not having the enthusiasm for yachting that she had for horse-racing, had on July 23 presented a cup—to be known as the Queen's Cup—to the New York Yacht Club for competition each year at the Newport, Rhode Island, Regatta in July. This replaced the King's Cup given to the Club by her father.

By August the plans for the Coronation were taking shape, and the Queen was already beginning to discuss the exact constitution of the service itself. She was also considering such important items as her gown, the gowns for her Maids of Honour and those peeresses attending in Westminster Abbey, the design of the special Coronation chairs, details of Coronation souvenirs, and the thousand and one other matters which take months of preparation before they reach fulfilment.

Mr Norman Hartnell, the Queen's dressmaker, was working on preliminary designs for the Queen's gown in his studio at Windsor. He had a regular audience with Her Majesty, and gradually the selected design emerged from more than a dozen ideas submitted.

The Queen was at Balmoral between August 8 and October 13. While there she entertained King Feisal II of Iraq and his uncle Abdel Illah. Her Majesty broke off her holiday to travel south to Doncaster on September 13 to watch Tulyar win the St Leger for the Aga Khan.

On September 30 it was announced in the *London*

Gazette that "The Queen has been graciously pleased . . . to declare and ordain that His Royal Highness, Philip, Duke of Edinburgh . . . shall henceforth upon all occasions and in all meetings, except where otherwise provided by Act of Parliament, have, hold, and enjoy place, pre-eminence, and precedence next to Her Majesty." That was an announcement which gave the greatest pleasure throughout the Commonwealth, and it certainly made it plain that at the Coronation Prince Philip would, after the Archbishop of Canterbury, be the first to render homage to the Queen after she had been enthroned.

Back at Buckingham Palace on October 15, the Queen gave daily audiences to visiting foreign diplomats, including M. Menderes, the Turkish Prime Minister, and M. Koprulu, the Foreign Minister, on October 15, and the Vietnamese Minister, who presented two gifts from the Emperor Bao Dai (one of them a portrait of Her Majesty) on October 16. Lieutenant-General Lord Freyberg, V.C., and Lady Freyberg lunched at the Palace on October 17 after Lord Freyberg had finally relinquished his appointment as Governor-General of New Zealand. On October 17 the Queen received Admiral Sir Geoffrey Oliver on the relinquishment of his post as Commander-in-Chief East Indies Station. On October 20 Admiral Sir John Edelsten, the retiring C.-in-C. Mediterranean, came to the Palace for an audience with Her Majesty.

Another famous sailor saw the Queen on October 21. He was Admiral Sir Dudley North, Admiral Commanding Northern Atlantic in 1940 when six French warships slipped through the Strait of Gibraltar in an escape bid from Toulon to Dakar. Admiral Sir Dudley North had been relieved of his command after that incident and had never ceased to demand an inquiry which would vindicate his name. His daughter, Miss Mary North, had become the nurse-governess to the three daughters of King Frederick of Denmark, and a few months before the Admiral was granted his audience with the Queen Miss North had been in London with the princesses when their father and mother paid a private visit. The three little girls stayed with the Duke and Duchess of Gloucester while in England. But it was to be five years after he had seen the Queen that the Admiral was to hear the Prime Minister, Mr Harold Macmillan, say publicly that no blame was attached to Sir Dudley North for the escape of the warships.

Lord Clarendon, the Lord Chamberlain, had retired from office on October 21, and the Queen had invested him with the Royal Victorian Chain in recognition of his long services in his high office. Lord Scarbrough took over the post and received the white wand and badge of office from the Queen at Buckingham Palace on October 27.

On October 29 the Queen received Dr Radhakrishnan, the Vice-President of the Republic of India, at the Palace, and their talk on the position and condition of Anglo-Indian relations was of the utmost importance. As Head of the Commonwealth the Queen occupies a position in the Indian Constitution that is without parallel in history. Her father was the last Emperor of India, and in a republic Her Majesty could have no power. Yet India's politicians have always recognized that she provides the only possible link between nations of different race, creed, and political views. The Queen has many times been the means of smoothing over differences between member nations of the Commonwealth since her accession. She can take action, detached from politics, where intervention by the Prime Minister and Government of Britain would be considered quite rightly an affront to national sovereignty.

Dr Fisher, the Archbishop of Canterbury, lunched with the Queen on November 6 after he had been received in audience half an hour earlier. At that audience the Coronation formed the major part of the discussion. The Queen discussed with the Archbishop the extent to which filming and televising of the ceremony itself could be allowed. She stressed the importance of the millions in Britain and many other countries being given the opportunity of 'being in' the Abbey during the service which had such great significance in British life. It was finally agreed that the cameras could be allowed to come east of the screen and into the actual Theatre where the Crowning would take place. Thus the Recognition, the Crowning, and the Homage would all be seen. Only the taking of Communion would be excluded.

The final selections of the design for the Queen's Coronation gown had been made by October, and in the middle of November the weaving of the velvet for her robe was begun at the mills of Warner and Sons, Ltd, Braintree, Essex. The cloth was woven by hand by Mrs Hilda Calver and Miss Lily Lee on a hand-loom identical with looms which have been in use for centuries. Two lengths were produced so that one could be kept in reserve against accidents to the first.

During November 1952 Prince Philip finally managed to find time to learn to fly—something he had been anxious to do for years. His first flight at White Waltham, Berkshire, on November 12 was greeted in some quarters with alarm. It was thought that the Prince was too much in the 'veteran' stage to become a pilot. But Prince Philip had talked the matter over with the Queen, and they were both agreed that if the vast and growing demands of their public duties were to be answered it was essential for both to achieve the utmost mobility. Thus the Queen, who is not an enthusiastic air traveller, nevertheless frequently chooses that form of transport because it alone allows her to crowd more engagements into a given period.

The Queen opened her first Parliament on November 4, when she drove in state to Westminster, and on the way provided for Press photographer Mr Charles Dawson an unforgettable picture of smiling pride which was published in almost every country in the world and in thousands of newspapers and magazines. I was in the United States at the time, and did not see a single newspaper which had not used the picture. People stopped me in the streets when they knew I was British and expressed their admiration for the Queen. The widespread publication of the photograph came to Her Majesty's notice, and she took the trouble to find out who had taken the picture. This revealed once more her determination always to keep abreast of everything that happens about her. This is a most well-developed trait of her character.

At the beginning of December the Queen was busy with the visit of the Ministers who had come to London for the Commonwealth Conference. Apart from receiving them in audience at the Palace, Her Majesty entertained seven Prime Ministers at a dinner in the State Dining Room on the first floor of the Palace on December 3. In this room are seven full-length royal portraits which occupy almost the whole of the wall facing the windows looking out over the gardens.

The Queen sat beneath the central portrait, Sir Thomas Lawrence's great nine-feet-high painting of King George IV, the builder of the Palace. Prince Philip, Queen Elizabeth the Queen Mother, Princess Margaret, the Duke and Duchess of Gloucester, the Princess Royal, the Duchess of Kent, Princess Alice Countess of Athlone, and the Earl of Athlone were also present.

It was the first big dinner party at which the Queen had presided at the Palace since her accession. The Prime Ministers present were: Mr Churchill; Mr Louis St Laurent, Canada; Mr Robert Menzies, Australia; Mr S. G. Holland, New Zealand; Mr K. Nazimuddin, Pakistan; Mr D. Senanayake, Ceylon; and Sir Godfrey Huggins, Southern Rhodesia. The Prime Ministers of India and South Africa, Mr Nehru and Mr Malan, who did not come to Britain for the conference, were represented by Mr Deshmukh and Mr Havenga, who also attended this dinner at the Palace.

On December 8 an announcement was made of alterations to the Coronation arrangements. The Queen had been discussing the matter of the route of the Coronation procession through London to and from the Abbey. She was anxious that it should be as extended as possible in order that as many people as could be crowded into the pavements and the overlooking buildings could see her progress. It was now announced that the route had been extended by the addition of Northumberland Avenue, Victoria Embankment, and Bridge Street so that many thousands of children could see the Queen go by. Four afternoon drives with Prince Philip through various parts of London were also announced, and several other visits and engagements after the Coronation.

From Sandringham on December 25 the Queen made her first traditional Christmas Day broadcast. Seated in the chair and at the desk in the study from which her father and grandfather had spoken to their peoples, Her Majesty said:

"Many grave problems and difficulties confront us, but with a new faith in the old and splendid beliefs given us by our forefathers, and the strength to venture beyond the safeties of the past, I know we shall be worthy of our duty.

"Above all we must keep alive that courageous spirit of adventure that is the finest quality of youth. . . .

"At my Coronation next June I shall dedicate myself anew to your service. I shall do so in the presence of a great congregation drawn from every part of the Commonwealth and Empire, while millions outside Westminster Abbey will hear the promises and prayers being offered up within its walls, and see much of the ancient ceremony in which kings and queens before me have taken part through century upon century. . . .

"I want to ask you all, whatever your religion may be, to pray for me on that day—to pray that God may give me wisdom and strength to carry out the solemn promises I shall be making and that I may faithfully serve Him, and you, all the days of my life."

The broadcast had an immediate effect throughout the world. "Elizabeth II of England faces a world so much more forbidding than that of her great predecessor, Elizabeth I, that we can only marvel at the courage with which, in her Christmas address to her people, she bade them display the strength to venture beyond the safeties of the past," declared the *Baltimore Sun.*

"Only the bold can be free. . . . She [Queen Elizabeth] believes, as we all must believe if we are not to degenerate to the status of slaves, that greatness of spirit survives in Western peoples, that by taking thought they can add cubits to their stature, that man faces a future more glorious than his past, however arduous the road he must follow," the paper added.

That was the basis of all comment—the courage of the new Queen.

8

Rehearsal in the Ballroom

CHRISTMAS holidays at Sandringham in 1952–53 came to an end on February 9. There had been more than usual to do, for the Queen and Prince Philip were already discussing plans for farming the estate even more intensively than it had been in the past.

While the Court was still at Sandringham the east coast of England was struck by the fierce gales and high tides which were to destroy so many homes and claim so many lives. At Sandringham about 7000 acres were flooded. On the Home Farm, owned and farmed by the Queen, 1000 acres were flooded and some stock were lost. A further 1200 acres were flooded on land belonging to the Queen but let to neighbouring farms. The winds did considerable damage to trees on the estate. So the Queen was a sufferer with the thousands of her subjects.

Since December many people had been speculating on the state of health of Queen Mary. The aged Queen had decided early in that month that she would not attend the Coronation ceremony the following June—a decision that must have caused her the greatest distress, for it would have been the proudest day of her life to be present in Westminster Abbey to see her granddaughter crowned. She would also have made history, for never has any British Queen Consort witnessed the Coronation of her grandchild.

As she drove in state to open Parliament on November 4, 1952, Her Majesty the Queen gave a waiting Press photographer this picture of smiling happiness which was published in newspapers and magazines all over the world.

Three studies of royal racing interest. At Epsom the Queen watches the horses approaching the stand. In her face there is first speculation, then dawning hope, and finally smiling delight, but not for yet another royal winner, for this was the 1957 Derby, and Her Majesty's Doutelle finished tenth.

But the death of King George VI had left an even greater mark on Queen Mary than was apparent. She had at last begun to age in spirit as well as in years. So it was with relief that the public was able to read the letter which she addressed to the Prime Minister on February 1 expressing her sympathy for those who had lost relatives and homes in the flood disaster, and to judge from that that all was well with her. "I am appalled by the accounts coming in of the extent of the havoc wrought by the terrible storm on Saturday night," she wrote. "My thoughts and my heartfelt sympathy are with all those who have suffered the loss of their nearest and dearest and the destruction of their homes and belongings in this overwhelming tragedy."

Without doubt her holiday at Sandringham had benefited Queen Mary. She returned to London on January 29, and was then seen about the capital on her afternoon drives. Queen Mary's granddaughter was more than ever busy behind the scenes with the preparations for her Coronation, but she had also a constant stream of visitors to see at the Palace. There were sittings for new portraits by artists—Dennis Fildes, Terence Cuneo, Mrs Gillick, and James Gunn—and photo sittings to Baron. Her Majesty welcomed the Sultan of Muscat on February 20. On March 17 she received Marshal Tito of Yugoslavia and entertained him to lunch at Buckingham Palace afterwards.

By this time the Queen and the rest of the Royal Family had the gravest fears for the health of Queen Mary. On March 2 it had been announced that Queen Mary had been confined to her bed for the preceding week by a recurrence of gastric trouble. Queen Elizabeth had visited her grandmother at Marlborough House during that week and had been assured that the illness was responding to treatment. But now there was cause for some alarm in view of Queen Mary's great age—almost eighty-six years. Queen Elizabeth gave orders that the Princess Royal, who was visiting the West Indies, and the Duke of Windsor, planning to come to London at the end of March, should be warned that their mother was ill.

On March 16 a report was issued that Queen Mary had experienced a less comfortable night and a less restful day, and immediately public concern mounted. This anxious time was followed by better news for some days, and by March 20 Queen Mary's doctors felt that it was possible to drop the frequent bulletins on her condition.

Two days later, however, Queen Mary, as if convinced that her end was near, expressed a wish to Queen Elizabeth that even if she were to die within a day or so of the Coronation no change should be made in the arrangements. This was fully in keeping with Queen Mary's character. All her life she had submerged her personal feelings in the overwhelming desire to serve the country and to do what she considered her duty. It was said of her that on one occasion, when she had been told that some distinguished public man had died, she exclaimed, "How careless of him to die in the middle of the season." Queen Mary's willpower had always been exceptional. On the day of the death of King George VI she had asked to be left alone in her room after having had her photo albums sent to her. All day long she sat with her memories of her son and her grief for him. When next she emerged she had her feelings completely under control.

Queen Elizabeth had a report early on March 24 that her grandmother had spent a disturbed night, and a general bulletin was issued from Marlborough House at 11.40 A.M.

"Queen Mary had a restless night due to a sudden occurrence of more severe symptoms of gastric trouble. Her Majesty's condition is causing some anxiety," it said. Queen Elizabeth received several telephone messages during the morning, and long before the second bulletin was issued at 1.40 P.M. Her Majesty knew that her grandmother's condition was now grave.

The Duchess of Kent called at Marlborough House fifty minutes after this bulletin was published, which said, "During the past hours Queen Mary's condition has become more grave. There has been a serious weakening of the heart action which gives rise to increasing anxiety."

The Duke of Windsor arrived five minutes later at 2.35 P.M., and when he left the Archbishop of Canterbury followed him in. Queen Elizabeth the Queen Mother reached Marlborough House at 3.09 P.M., and at 4.46 P.M. the Queen, Prince Philip, and Princess Margaret arrived together. Towards 6 P.M. the Duke and Duchess of Gloucester arrived, and they were followed by the Duke of Windsor, who stayed, the watching crowd were quick to notice, only ten minutes.

At 7 P.M. another bulletin announced, "Queen Mary's strength is ebbing, but Her Majesty is sleeping peacefully."

The Princess Royal was at Marlborough House when her mother died at 10.20 P.M., and the Duke of Windsor drove up ten minutes later.

The waiting crowd of 500 outside saw, through the darkness and the fog that surrounded the great house, the personal standard of Queen Mary, the Arms of the United Kingdom incorporating the Arms of Teck, come fluttering down from the masthead above the roof. As the last falling leaf marks the end of autumn, the lowered standard marked the end of an era.

The tributes to Queen Mary were world-wide and wonderful. In a moving broadcast tribute Mr Winston Churchill expressed the sorrow of "men and women of all ages in life, in all lands owning allegiance to the Crown." He said, "During six reigns—far longer, that is, than most people can remember—she has moved among us with the poise and dignity which, as age drew on, made her a figure of almost legendary distinction.

"She died in the knowledge that the Crown of these realms, worn so gloriously by her husband and by her son and so soon to be set with all solemnity on the head of her granddaughter, is far more broadly and securely based on the people's love and the nation's will than in the sedate days of her youth, when rank and privilege ruled society."

Almost every one had memories of the great lady who could be so imperious and yet so human. I remembered most being present at a Fakenham, Norfolk, antique shop when she was there. A bullock from the market broke away from its captors and raced through the streets. Balked by a line of men, the fear-crazed animal swerved to one side and charged in through the door of the shop, scattering the antique china and furniture.

The occupants of the shop, including myself, dived for cover—except one, Queen Mary. I saw her raise her lorgnettes to her eyes, and her hand held her parasol stiffly before her. It did not quiver and was like an imperious sword. The animal stopped, pawed the floor, and was seized and secured by the market men and led away.

We all came sheepishly from our hiding-places, and Queen Mary, voice steady and untroubled, continued with her inspection of the pieces on display.

Apart from her family and friends, of course, there was no greater love in Queen Mary's life than beautiful silverware and furniture, Chinese jade, fans from all countries, snuffboxes, clocks, and other products of the craftsmen. She was an acknowledged international expert in all these things and, apart from her work at Buckingham Palace on the treasures there, she had filled Marlborough House with some of the rarest examples of Georgian silver and furniture, jade, and *objets d'art* to be found in any house in Britain. She was an indefatigable collector, and could think of no better way of spending a free moment than in browsing through some antique shop or collection.

Queen Mary was known to antique dealers in many parts. On one occasion she was looking through a Windsor shop, while in residence at the Castle, and found a piece which interested her. She inquired how much it was, and, being told £9, offered instead £6. The dealer refused to alter his price, respectfully reminding Her Majesty that the piece was worth every penny of the money asked. The Queen returned to the Castle and sat silent for some moments in her sitting-room. Then quietly she asked her closest friend and lady-in-waiting, Lady Cynthia Colville, to telephone the shop and say that she would have the piece after all. "And you had better pay him his nine pounds," Queen Mary said, "although I still do not think it is worth it."

On the morning following Queen Mary's death the Queen inspected the first of the specially designed Coronation straight-backed chairs with blue velour upholstery on which was embroidered in gold the cipher E II R. Queen Mary had seen and expressed her approval of the design, and a specimen would certainly have been added to her collection had she lived. The Queen had had the chairs set out at the Palace in the Caernarvon Room, the private dining-room of the Belgian Suite, which she and Prince Philip were still occupying.

Queen Mary's funeral took place in St George's Chapel, Windsor, on March 31. In the place where the banners of chivalry hung still as the grey stone vaulting above them the aged Queen's body was lowered into the Royal vaults. Queen Mary's banner of arms covered the coffin and went down into the depths with it as the young Queen Elizabeth sprinkled dust three times upon it from that same bowl from which she had taken the dust that she had sifted lightly upon her father's coffin in the same place just a year before. The choir had sung unaccompanied Queen Mary's favourite hymn, "Abide with Me," but the organ joined in to lead the last triumphant singing of "Glorious Things of Thee are spoken."

Outside, the lawns were massed with the floral tributes of half the world, but it was significant of the place that Queen Mary held in British life that the tiny tributes of the humble people vastly outnumbered the gorgeous wreaths of the great.

The Queen and Prince Philip, who had gone into residence at Windsor Castle on March 30, remained there after the funeral. Her Majesty travelled to London to distribute the Royal Maundy money at St Paul's Cathedral on April 2—a ceremony which, in the previous March, had been the first official function of her reign, and one whose symbolism she regards as of first importance. The Maundy money had normally been distributed from Westminster Abbey in previous years, but on this occasion, owing to the preparation for the Coronation, Her Majesty distributed it at St Paul's Cathedral. At 2.30 on the same day the Queen received King Hussein of Jordan at Buckingham Palace, and returned with Prince Philip to Windsor Castle in the evening.

While at Windsor Queen Elizabeth was able to follow the progress of the work on her Coronation gown and robe with greater ease, for Mr Norman Hartnell could come over at a moment's notice from his Windsor home. There were much more than the usual considerations of the design when the dress was being planned. The need for movement on the part of Her Majesty during the long and involved service, the necessity to keep to the minimum the weight she must carry, the state of lighting in the Abbey, and particularly in the Theatre itself, the predominant colours of the rich vestments that would be worn during the ceremony, and the colours surrounding —all these points had to be taken into account.

On April 15 Prince Philip attended a meeting of the Royal Mint Sub-committee at which the design of the new Great Seal was finally accepted, and afterwards he drove to the studio in Pembroke Walk, Kensington, of Mr Gilbert Ledward, the sculptor, to discuss the design. It was Mr Ledward who had designed the effigy of the Queen mounted on Winston, the police horse, used for the Coronation celebration five-shilling piece. The Prince was back in Windsor for dinner, and he boarded the Royal train at 10 P.M. with the Queen at the start of the visit to Scotland, which included a call at Dumbarton before the naming of the new royal yacht, built in the yard of John Brown.

There had been much speculation on the name Her Majesty would reveal when the ship first slid down the launching ways. At the moment the yacht was just a number, and few knew the name the Queen had selected. Some said that the new ship would perpetuate the *Victoria and Albert* name of the royal yachts. Others thought that *Elizabeth and Philip* would be the chosen name. When the Queen announced in ringing tones, "I name this ship *Britannia*," there was an audible gasp of surprise from the crowd and then a great gust of cheering.

On April 24 the Queen, again in residence at Windsor Castle, made the Prime Minister a Knight of the Garter and invested him with the insignia of the Order. Sir Winston Churchill was the first commoner to receive the Garter since its award was placed within the sole prerogative of the sovereign on December 4, 1946. In the seventeenth century the Order had been seized by the victorious leaders of the Glorious Revolution and used both by the Whigs and the Tories to reward their supporters and friends. It was for this reason—that it was a political award—that Sir Winston Churchill had refused the honour when it was first offered him in 1945. After it had been removed from politics he accepted it at the hands of the Queen.

Sir Winston was invested by the Queen, but his installation was not immediately possible. It was later announced that the badge of the Garter that the Prime Minister would wear at the Coronation would be the "Greater George," the badge, double normal size, which had been presented by Queen Anne to Sir Winston's famous ancestor, the Duke of Marlborough, after his successful campaigns on the Continent. On Marlborough's death the badge had returned to royal keeping, but was presented by the Prince Regent, later King George IV, to the Duke of Wellington in 1813. On the Duke's death, as a special mark of distinction for his services, his family was allowed to retain the badge and not return it as is customary. It had been kept in Apsley House (now the Wellington Museum), and it was on the suggestion of the present Duke of Wellington that it was brought out for Sir Winston's use.

After the ceremony in the Green Drawing Room at Windsor Sir Winston and Lady Churchill accompanied the Queen and Prince Philip to dinner in their private dining-room. After dinner the party returned to the Green Drawing Room for the remainder of the evening and a constant stream of reminiscences of his seventy-eight years from the great Parliamentarian. Sir Winston and Lady Churchill stayed the night at Windsor Castle.

One thousand Scouts came to Windsor Castle on April 26 to march past the Queen and Prince Philip. They were Queen's Scouts and holders of Scouts' awards for gallantry. The Dean of Windsor conducted a service for them in St George's Chapel.

There was a very good reason for the long residence at Windsor Castle. Buckingham Palace, while the Queen and Prince Philip were in the country, was being got ready for the Coronation season. The great State rooms—the Ballroom, the Dining Room, the famous Balcony Room and the balcony itself, the Bow Room, the Throne Room—were all being spring cleaned. Paintwork and furnishings, carpets and curtaining—all had to be made ready for the great days immediately ahead. In the Palace Mews the Coronation coach was overhauled and regilded. In the workrooms in the basement the famous Royal gold plate, the priceless glass and china, were inspected and made ready. In the kitchens the Queen's chef, M. Aubrey, planned the menus for banquets and lunches, even prepared plans for the snack lunch that the Queen and the Royal Family would take in Westminster Abbey after the ceremony and before the drive back to the Palace began.

The Queen and Prince Philip had been driven round the

Palace Courtyard seated in the gold coach drawn by eight magnificent greys. As a treat Prince Charles and Princess Anne, who had been watching the rehearsal, were taken for a complete circuit of the Courtyard. When lifted down again Princess Anne alarmed every one by suddenly darting between the rear wheels to try to turn the huge brake wheel.

For Prince Philip May 4 was a most important day. At 2.30 P.M. on that day he was presented with his wings by the Chief of the Air Staff, Air Marshal [later Marshal of the Royal Air Force] Sir William Dickson. Three days later the Prince was presented with his Field-Marshal's baton by the Queen at a private ceremony in her own study at the Palace.

While at Windsor Castle the Queen had studied the involved ceremonial of the Coronation service, and, back at Buckingham Palace on May 1, she began a series of rehearsals in the White Drawing Room, once the Music Room of Prince Albert, the Prince Consort. In this room is the famous 'secret' door into the Royal Closet (a small private drawing-room), which on one occasion was the only thing about Buckingham Palace which interested one wealthy princely visitor from India. The door is formed by one of four ebony cabinets filled with lovely china and surmounted by identical tall, gilded mirrors.

For her rehearsals the Queen had records of the Coronation of her father played on a radiogram in the room, and carefully she went through each phase of the service. The White Drawing Room, being not so different in size from the Theatre in Westminster Abbey in which the Coronation would take place, was ideal for the purpose, for actual distances could be measured in order that the Queen might judge exactly how fast she should walk and the length and number of steps necessary to get her from station to station at the right moment of the service.

Later the magnificent white-and-gold State Ballroom of the Palace was marked out as an exact replica—from the point of view of distances—of the Abbey from West Door to Theatre. There the Queen was able to rehearse timing from the moment when, as she entered the West Door of the Abbey, the choir would sing the anthem "I was glad when they said unto me, We will go into the House of the Lord," and the Queen's Scholars of Westminster School greeted Her Majesty with their "Vivats," until she reached her Chair of Estate in the Theatre, when the service proper would begin.

There were many official engagements to keep during May. On May 2 the Queen and Prince Philip saw Blackpool beat Bolton Wanderers in the F.A. Cup Final at Wembley. On May 4 there was a Presentation Party at Buckingham Palace. On the same afternoon a deputation of the Wardens and Clerk of the Girdlers Company presented the Queen with a sword-belt and stock. On May 5 the Queen laid the foundation stone of the new building of the Royal College of Surgeons. At noon on that day she received the Crown Prince of Japan, who had come to London to attend the Coronation.

The Queen and Prince Philip attended a gala performance of *Henry VIII* at the Old Vic on May 6, and there was a second Presentation Party at Buckingham Palace on May 7. In the afternoon the Queen and Prince Philip were visited by Prince Mohammed Ali of Egypt, a cousin of King Farouk, who came to pay his personal respects and to express regrets that General Neguib, the Egyptian dictator, had decided not to be represented at the Coronation.

On May 8 the Queen, accompanied by Prince Philip, presided at a meeting of the Prince's Council at the Duchy of Cornwall Office in Buckingham Gate. Between May 8 and May 17 the Queen was in residence at Balmoral, and immediately on her return to London she received Major-General J. A. Gascoigne at Buckingham Palace. He was in command of the London District, and had the responsibility of the troops along the Coronation route and of the billeting arrangements at Pirbright and Woolwich. The Queen discussed with General Gascoigne the general arrangements for the welfare of the troops and the visits Prince Philip was making to the camps. On May 26 the Prince flew direct by helicopter from the Buckingham Palace lawns to Pirbright camp, where General Gascoigne was awaiting him with 2000 Commonwealth troops.

Final details of the ball to be given in her honour by the Officers of the Household Brigade on May 30 were also presented to Her Majesty by General Gascoigne at the Buckingham Palace meeting.

The Commonwealth Parliamentary Association was to have been host to the Queen at a luncheon in Westminster Hall on May 27, but the Association's council instead asked that all fifty-two Commonwealth Parliaments represented in the Association should act as joint hosts. The Queen was delighted at this suggestion. It enabled her to refer to the unique quality of the occasion that the representatives of all fifty-two Parliaments, which had grown out of the original body which had met in Westminster Hall seven centuries before, could now meet together.

Because the Palace of Westminster is a royal palace Her Majesty herself presided, although she was guest of honour, and Mr Harold Holt, Australia's Minister of Labour, chairman of the Association's General Council, officiated. And because by ancient precedent the Lord Great Chamberlain and the Minister of Works have the right to greet the sovereign visiting Westminster Hall, they performed that duty and not her hosts.

Rehearsals at Westminster Abbey for the Coronation were now in full swing. On Sunday, May 10, the State coach which the Queen would use was driven along the entire route. On May 17 a second rehearsal of the drive took place. On May 14 there was a first and private rehearsal of the ceremony inside the Abbey. This enabled the Abbey clergy who would carry the Regalia from the Jerusalem Chamber, where it would repose overnight on the eve of the Coronation, to the annexe at the West Door to practise their parts.

On May 15 the Duchess of Norfolk, acting as stand-in for the Queen, took part with the Archbishop of Canterbury in the Abbey in a rehearsal of the Coronation. Sir Eric Miéville, a former assistant secretary to King George VI, took the place of Prince Philip. Again on May 18 the Bishops and High Officers of State rehearsed the carrying of the Regalia. On May 19 the Duchess of Norfolk again took part in a rehearsal at the Abbey, this time for the ceremony of the Anointing.

Queen Elizabeth visited the Abbey on May 21 to watch further rehearsals—the Homage and the Oblation of an ingot of gold and an altar cloth. The Duchess of Norfolk was again Her Majesty's stand-in.

On May 22 the Queen took part in a rehearsal at the Abbey for the first time when she practised the difficult section of the service described in the Rubric as "The Queen shall descend from her Throne, supported and attended as before, where, delivering her Crown and Sceptre and Rod to the Lord Great Chamberlain or other appointed Officers to hold, she shall kneel down." Rehearsed also was the Recess—that point in the service where the Queen was to be divested of her red Robe Royal and be clothed in its place with her Robe of purple velvet, in which, and wearing the Imperial Crown, she would leave the Abbey to enter her golden State coach at the end of the service.

The Queen had decided to wear St Edward's Crown for the Coronation, despite its great weight, and she wore it during a long rehearsal of the ceremony on May 27.

On the following day Queen Elizabeth the Queen Mother and Princess Margaret rehearsed the procession to their seats in the Abbey.

And so, on May 29, to the final 'dress rehearsal' in the Abbey, in which, it had been rumoured, the Queen and other members of the Royal Family would take part. But the packed Abbey and the great crowd outside were disappointed. The Queen's rehearsals at 'home' in Buckingham Palace were considered adequate, and the Duchess of Norfolk took her place and heard her husband afterwards pay tribute to a "superb performance."

On May 30 there was a Government reception to the Commonwealth and other overseas guests, and on June 1 the Queen gave a reception and luncheon to the Commonwealth Prime Ministers and representatives. And now it seemed that all the world had in truth turned its eyes to London.

9

Coronation

THE London streets were filled with people before dawn on June 2, 1953—people hurrying through the rain and the unsummerlike cold to get to some vantage point they had selected from which to view the Coronation procession. There was nothing but anticipation to keep their spirits high until the news began to spread that the British Himalayan Expedition had conquered Everest. That was taken as a good omen for the day and the reign.

Throughout the night thousands of people had trudged through the streets of London, which had been transformed for the occasion—streets with arches stretching from pavement to pavement, streets gay with bunting and flags, streets colourful with flowers. There was a feeling of excitement and tension in the air. In front of the darkened Palace the crowds assembled, their thoughts entirely of the Queen who would soon be rising to prepare for the day. The waiting throng were chilled and wet and hungry, yet their talk was all of the great day that lay ahead.

I left home at 3.30 A.M. to make sure I should get to my seat in the North Triforium of the Abbey before the doors were closed at 6.30 A.M. I presented my ticket and climbed the worn stone stairs, and suddenly was in a confined space filled almost to the stone ceiling with tier upon tier of rough wooden benches. I slid into the place marked for me and faced a blank grey wall in which some long-forgotten stonemason had carved a hole shaped something like a Tudor rose.

The form was hard. Already I was pondering on the inescapable fact that I would have to sit there for eleven hours. And I had been warned that there was little chance that I should see anything of the Coronation. Through the circular opening in front of me I could see the seats of the peers in the South Transept stretching up towards the South Triforium. They were empty as yet.

Time passed slow as a funeral march. From somewhere away to my right a hidden orchestra, undoubtedly the 400 selected musicians from all the Commonwealth who were ensconced somewhere above the screen, began to play softly.

I leaned forward to ease my cramped position. With almost a shock of surprise I found that there in front of my eyes—framed by the rounded artistry of that medieval mason—was the whole of the Theatre. I could see St Edward's Chair—standing before the High Altar on its gilded lions and holding the Stone of Destiny, on which kings and queens have been crowned for centuries in the islands of the United Kingdom. I could see Her Majesty's Chair of Estate standing in front of the Royal Gallery, whose façade was made beautiful by the wonderful gold plate of Westminster Abbey. In full view was the Throne itself, standing on a golden daïs in the centre of the Area, and also the chairs for the royal dukes at the south-west corner.

The discomfort of my seat was forgotten. Here was a view that could not be bettered in all the Abbey. I knew that from the time the Queen entered the Theatre for her

Recognition until the supreme moment of the Coronation, when all the thousands would render homage to Queen Elizabeth, Her Majesty would not be out of my sight. I realized that the seats opposite were beginning to fill up. The surging whispers of hundreds of people reached up to us in the Triforium as everywhere the invited congregation took their seats before the doors were closed at 8.30 A.M. Through my circular observation hole I could see the peers arriving in the gorgeous robes of their orders of chivalry, their colours eclipsing the gowns of the peeresses but not dimming the glittering magnificence of the women's tiaras.

There were occasional diversions. I saw a begowned figure enter the Theatre and sit close under the Royal Gallery. Presently he reached his hand under his gown and produced an evening newspaper. Then he proceeded to study the back page.

The Triforium immediately above the altar was empty of seats and guarded by a single Gold Stick. We suddenly noticed that a door at the back wall had opened, and a single file of white-clad cleaners and cloakroom attendants came through to tiptoe to the edge to look down into the Theatre. Gold Stick immediately ordered them out and stood guard at the door. Almost immediately a second door farther away along the wall opened and the little group reappeared, and again tiptoed to the edge of the Theatre to watch what was going on below. It was some time before Gold Stick noticed and again cleared the area.

Soon after the arrival in the Royal Gallery of the Queen Mother and Princess Margaret a little procession of four cleaners with carpet-sweepers and a broom filed into the Theatre and proceeded to sweep the golden carpet round the Throne.

Time was not important now. But soon I was watching the 'junior' members of the Royal Family taking their places in the Royal Gallery—the Harewoods, the Cambridges, the Mountbattens, and the Marquess of Milford Haven. A word passed along the line of hard forms in the Triforium announced that the foreign dignitaries were filing into their seats in the Choir—the Crown Prince of Norway; Prince George of Greece; Prince Axel of Denmark; Prince Bertil of Sweden; Prince Albert of Liège; Prince Bernhard of the Netherlands; M. Georges Bidault, representing France; General George Marshall, of the U.S.A.; M. Jacob Malik, the representative of Soviet Russia. Eighty-one visiting celebrities came to their places, then the representatives of Her Majesty's protectorates, including the colourful Queen Salote of Tonga, in red—with a red feather in her hat—and the rulers of the Malay States.

There was movement directly below me. I saw the Dean and Prebendaries bearing the Regalia assembling at the High Altar. Led by the choir, they carried the priceless symbols of kingship, which had been stored overnight in the Jerusalem Chamber, away out of sight, to the Vestibule without the West Door, to await the arrival of Her Majesty.

Now the Princes and Princesses of the Blood Royal began to file into their seats in the Royal Gallery—the Princess Royal; the Duchess of Gloucester and her children; the Duchess of Kent with Princess Alexandra and Prince Michael; Princess Alice Countess of Athlone and the Earl of Athlone; Lady Patricia Ramsay; and Princess Marie Louise. They were followed by the processions of Queen Elizabeth the Queen Mother and Princess Margaret, who sat in the front row of the Royal Gallery with a vacant seat between them. That told me that later Prince Charles would be coming to see his mother crowned.

Now there was a stir of excitement in the Abbey. The hands of watches were pointing to 10.45, and somewhere outside the golden State coach bearing the Queen and Prince Philip was rolling on through the wet streets towards the Abbey. At eleven o'clock word came along the rows of seats that the Queen and Prince Philip had arrived and were being greeted by the Earl Marshal and the other Great Officers of State, the Archbishops of Canterbury and York, and the Bishops her Supporters.

Another fifteen minutes passed, and gradually the excited clamour of the congregation was stilled. Here was the moment all the world was waiting for. Almost before anyone realized it the lovely opening notes of the anthem "I was glad whey they said unto me, We will go into the House of the Lord," were echoing through the church. A little prickle of excitement coursed along my spine, and the shrill cries of the Westminster scholars in their "Vivat Regina Elizabetha" were almost a jarring note.

How long we had to wait I could not say. But suddenly, without any warning, the Queen was there below me, framed in my observation window—a lovely picture in diamond diadem and in a robe of crimson velvet trimmed with ermine and bordered with gold lace. Her Majesty was wearing the collar of the Garter.

With firm and measured step—as she had practised so often in her own home—she moved to the faldstool before her Chair of Estate, and prayed. While the Queen prayed the peers who had charge of the Regalia came forward one by one to hand them to the Archbishop of Canterbury, standing on the altar steps. Lord Hastings and Lord Churston delivered St Edward's Staff, and

Viscount Cunningham of Hyndhope, the Lord High Steward, handed to the Archbishop St Edward's Crown, which the Queen—unlike most recent monarchs—had decided to use throughout the Coronation, despite its weight of more than five pounds. Now to the right of the Queen stood the Duke of Buccleuch with the Pointed Sword of Justice, the Duke of Northumberland with the Curtana (Sword of Mercy), the Marquess of Salisbury with the Sword of State.

The Queen rose from her faldstool. All the temporal power represented by the Regalia was now in the keeping of the Church. The moment had come for the Archbishop of Canterbury gradually to transfer that power to its rightful owner.

I watched as Garter King of Arms led the Archbishop, with the Lord Chancellor, Lord Great Chamberlain, Lord High Constable, and Earl Marshal, to the East Side of the Theatre. Behind me I could almost feel the massed rows of French, American, and German journalists stiffen as they realized that a great moment had come. The Archbishop, in ringing tones, called to the East, "Sirs, I here present unto you Queen Elizabeth, your undoubted Queen. Wherefore, all you who are come this day to do your homage and service, are you willing to do the same?" From behind me came the joyous cries of "God save Queen Elizabeth."

Each time the Recognition followed—in the South, the West, and finally on our own side, the North—the newspapermen from abroad joined in shouting acclamations to the Queen as the trumpets sounded fanfares.

The Oath of Service and the Presenting of the Bible followed, with the Moderator of the General Assembly of the Church of Scotland in rich, round tones declaring,

The Queen of Canada with Prince Philip drives in State in an open carriage to open her Canadian Parliament in Ottawa.

Royal Canadian Air Force Photo

"Here is wisdom; this is the royal law; these are the lively Oracles of God." The Queen's face was pale and composed, and not a quiver showed in her hands as she delivered back the Bible to the Moderator for its restoration to the altar.

And suddenly the whole great church was filled with the thrilling, triumphant notes of Handel's setting of "Zadok the Priest and Nathan the Prophet anointed Solomon King; and all the people rejoiced and said: God save the king, Long live the king, May the king live for ever, Amen. Hallelujah," words which have been used in unbroken sequence at every crowning in England from the Coronation of King Edgar the Peaceful at Bath in 973. While the blood-stirring Hallelujahs lifted in a crescendo the Queen was disrobed for the most solemn act of her Coronation—the Anointing.

Her Majesty herself took the diamond diadem from her head, as if unwilling to trust her hair-do to another, and handed it to the Mistress of the Robes. The great train was detached from the Queen's shoulders and folded backward by each pair of Maids of Honour, until it was a rich crimson pile overflowing the extended arms of the Groom of the Robes.

The Queen removed her jewellery piece by piece, divesting herself of every symbol of wealth and distinction, and at last, dressed only in a simple white garment, she took her seat in St Edward's Chair. Although it has been widely reported that Her Majesty forgot to remove her pearl drop earrings this is not so. It was never intended that she should remove them.

I became aware of movement at the back of the Royal Gallery, and presently a little figure in oyster satin suit, a Coronation medal pinned to his shirt, appeared, and was led down the steps to the front, where the Queen Mother and Princess Margaret greeted him. Prince Charles, his fair hair slicked down for the first time with brilliantine, perched himself on the edge of his seat and fixed his gaze firmly and unwaveringly on his mother. Only for the fraction of a second did I see the Queen's eyes flicker sideways for one swift glance at her son.

The little boy was not still for long. Soon the glitter of the gold plate attracted his attention, and in a moment he was hanging over the edge of the Royal Gallery, inspecting it. The Queen Mother hauled him back. A little later he disappeared from sight altogether, and I saw his grandmother and his aunt bending their heads, talking cogently to him. Still he did not reappear, and I could see that the Queen Mother was scraping one foot sideways and saying something with some urgency to her grandson. And presently, like a rocket, Prince Charles shot into view again, the Queen Mother's handbag triumphantly clasped in one small hand. After that he was still again on his seat and watched the service closely, asking questions of his grandmother and Princess Margaret and vigorously nodding his head at their answers.

Four Knights of the Garter in their beautiful mantles of blue velvet came from their seats among the peers and took from the Heralds the Canopy of Cloth of Gold, which they held over the Queen. But Her Majesty was still in full view to me through my observation window. The Archbishop came towards the Queen from the altar with the Dean bearing the silver-gilt eagle which formed the ampulla and the spoon of anointing, the most ancient of all the pieces of Regalia.

Dr Fisher's voice came to us as we craned forward in the Triforium: "Be thy hands anointed with holy oil, be thy breast anointed with holy oil, be thy head anointed with holy oil: as kings, priests, and prophets were anointed," he said.

I saw the Queen kneeling before the Archbishop as the blessing was said over her: ". . . that by the assistance of His heavenly grace you may govern and preserve the peoples committed to your charge in wealth, peace, and godliness; and after a long and glorious course of ruling a temporal kingdom wisely, justly, and religiously you may at last be made partaker of an eternal kingdom. . . ." Now Queen Elizabeth II was Queen indeed.

The Dean of Westminster, with the assistance of the Mistress of the Robes, put on Her Majesty the Colobium Sindonis, a sleeveless garment, and the Supertunica of cloth of gold, and the girdle.

Here was the beginning of the richest symbolism that exists in any land. The Lord Great Chamberlain on his knees presented Her Majesty with the golden spurs of St George, the symbols of knighthood, and the Queen touched them before they were taken back to the altar. The Marquis of Salisbury exchanged the huge Sword of State for a lighter weapon in a jewelled scabbard, and this the Archbishop put into the hand of the Queen: "Receive this kingly sword, brought now from the Altar of God. . . . With this sword do justice, stop the growth of iniquity, protect the holy Church of God, help and defend the widows and orphans, restore the things that are gone to decay, maintain the things that are restored, punish and reform what is amiss, and confirm what is in good order."

The Queen rose and walked to the altar and offered the sword in its scabbard to the Archbishop, who received it as a symbol that the Queen was offering up her temporal power to God. And Lord Salisbury, when Her Majesty had returned to St Edward's Chair, went himself to the altar with an embroidered bag containing 100 shillings, and with this redeemed the sword in accordance with custom. Drawing the sword from its scabbard, Lord Salisbury thereafter carried it naked before the Queen for the rest of the ceremony.

I watched the presentation of the gold bracelets, or armills, these being a gift of the Commonwealth Governments, but whose purpose still remains obscure. The Archbishop described them as "symbols and pledges of that bond which unites you with your peoples."

Now the Queen was garbed in the Stole and Robe Royal, a garment of cloth of gold and so magnificent as to be almost breathtaking. As I looked down on the scene I could see upon it the embroidered emblems of the countries of the United Kingdom. "The Lord clothe you with the robe of righteousness," said Dr Fisher, the Archbishop.

As Her Majesty sat in St Edward's Chair, all the other symbols of her authority were brought one by one from the altar. The Orb was delivered into the Queen's right hand with the words, "Remember that the whole world is subject to the power and empire of Christ." The Queen's ring, in which are a sapphire and a ruby, was placed on the fourth finger of Her Majesty's right hand. "Receive the ring of kingly dignity," said the Archbishop. "As you are this day consecrated to be our Head and Prince, so may you continue steadfastly as the Defender of Christ's Religion." The Sceptre and the Cross and the Rod with the Dove were handed to the Archbishop. At that moment Lord Woolton came out from his seat among the peers, and I saw him present a rich glove to Her Majesty—the ancient right of the tenants in serjeanty of the Manor of Worksop, and now symbolizing that authority must always be exercised with gentleness.

The Sceptre was placed in the Queen's right hand and the Rod in her left—the Sceptre as the ensign of power and justice, the Rod as the symbol of equity and mercy. "Be so merciful that you be not too remiss; so execute justice that you forget not mercy. Punish the wicked, protect and cherish the just, and lead your people in the way wherein they should go," prayed the Archbishop.

Behind me the listening newspapermen sensed that the great moment had come. As one man they rose in their seats. I kept my eyes to the opening and saw the Queen Mother in the Royal Gallery raise her hand swiftly and for one brief moment to her forehead. Princess Margaret seemed tense with emotion.

The Queen herself took one half-checked glance towards the Royal Gallery. In her right hand was the Sceptre, the Great Star of Africa, the largest cut diamond in the world, shining in its head; in her left hand the Rod with the Dove.

And on the altar the lovely St Edward's Crown, the crown made for Charles II at the Restoration. St Edward's Crown is of gold encrusted with diamonds, emeralds, and rubies, with drop pearl pendants hanging from the jewelled cross at its top. Now solitary at the altar, it blazed in the lights that beat upon it.

The Archbishop stood before the altar: "O God, the Crown of the faithful, bless, we beseech Thee, this Crown, and so sanctify Thy servant Elizabeth, upon whose head this day Thou dost place it for a sign of royal majesty, that she may be filled by Thine abundant grace with all princely virtues." This was the first time since the revision of the Coronation in 1685 that the Archbishop officiating had blessed the Crown or any material object. In 1685, before his Coronation, King James II, who had become a

Roman Catholic, gave instructions to the Protestant Archbishop Sancroft that the service should be abridged to conform as closely as possible to his beliefs. Sancroft recast all the prayers so that the blessing of the Regalia, as mentioned in the *Liber Regalis* in 1307, was transferred from the objects themselves to the King who would be invested with them. The restoring of former practice in this respect had been decided by the Queen and the Archbishop in their meetings in the months preceding the Coronation. Her Majesty had from the outset wished the service to conform most closely with the form used since ancient times, and this return to the form of the *Liber Regalis* was a natural outcome of that desire.

There was a hush throughout the Abbey. The silence was absolute as the Dean carried the Crown from the altar. The bishops and the lords attending the Queen gathered round St Edward's Chair. I saw Her Majesty's eyes lift as the Archbishop held the Crown high above her head. A flutter of movement came from the peers' gallery. Slowly, solemnly, the Archbishop brought the Crown down on to the Queen's head.

A great gust of sound swept up and through the Abbey and rolled about the vaulted roof. "God save the Queen," the people cried, again and again, and the trumpets blared in triumph. The princes and princesses, the peers and the peeresses, put on their coronets and caps and the Kings of Arms their crowns. And from behind me came a cry of "Dieu bénisse notre reine" (God save our Queen). It was that kind of moment.

Outside the bells were pealing, and softly, as if it were distant thunder, came the spontaneous cheering of the crowds and the salute of guns.

And soon the Queen went up to her Throne, to be lifted

into it by the Archbishops and bishops and peers of the kingdom. The Great Officers of State with the Swords and the Sceptres, and the lords who had carried the other Regalia, stood round the steps of the Throne while the Archbishop said, "Stand firm, and hold fast from henceforth the seat and state of royal and imperial dignity. . . . And the Lord God Almighty . . . establish your Throne in righteousness, that it may stand fast for evermore . . ."

This was the moment of the Homage. Now the Archbishop, who had for an hour past divested the Queen of all the badges of authority and returned them to her one by one, knelt at her feet, and as he knelt so did all the bishops, promising to "be faithful and true."

The page of the Earl Marshal came forward beside the Throne, a cushion in his hands, and one by one the peers, led by Prince Philip and the royal dukes, came forward, removed coronet and placed it on the cushion before mounting the steps of the Throne to do homage. Prince Philip swore in ancient feudal form to "become your liege man of life and limb, and of earthly worship; and faith and truth I will bear unto you, to live and die, against all manner of folks. So help me God." Rising, the Prince touched the Crown with his hand and kissed the Queen's left cheek. In doing so he touched the Crown with his head, and it slipped slightly to one side. The Duke of Gloucester followed, and then the Duke of Kent, who made only the mistake of forgetting to remove his gloves. Then the senior peer of each degree—Dukes, Marquesses, Earls, Viscounts, and Barons—in order came to give homage, and as each knelt before the Throne, so all the peers in his degree knelt in their places in the gallery. While this was going on the choir sang five anthems.

Now again the acclamations, every one crying aloud,

"God save Queen Elizabeth. Long live Queen Elizabeth. May the Queen live for ever." And once more my French friends cried, "Vive notre reine."

Prince Charles was moving unwillingly up the steps of the Royal Gallery, turning again and again for another look at his mother on her Throne, but at last he was gone from sight. The congregation sang:

> All people that on earth do dwell,
> Sing to the Lord with cheerful voice.

The Queen received Communion at the steps of the altar, and Her Majesty made her Oblation of an altar cloth and an ingot of gold weighing one pound.

The Communion ended, the Queen rose and received again her Crown, and, taking the Sceptre and the Rod into her hands, returned to her Throne. The choir began to sing the *Te Deum*—a sign that the Coronation was over. Her Majesty came down from her Throne, and with Sceptre and Rod in hands went slowly past the altar and into St Edward's Chapel beyond, with all the Regalia following her.

We sat down again and watched the formation of the procession that would lead Her Majesty out of the Abbey and into the rain and cold of the streets that the love of the millions gathered there would still make warm for their Queen. In her rest-room the Queen ate a fragment of sandwich and sipped a glass of wine. She was too filled with the emotion of the moment to eat much. Like all of us, she waited for the next great move.

Colour and pageantry passed before my eyes again as the robes and the uniforms and the banners and coronets went out as they had come in. And at last into the frame of my observation window was the Queen herself with

Prince Philip, Her Majesty regal and proud in her gorgeous Robe of purple velvet. And all the people sang with a fervour that can rarely have been matched, "God save our gracious Queen," until she was gone from sight, and sound died away.

How much the personality and bearing of the Queen had sustained us all through the weary hours of confinement was now apparent: we were hungry and thirsty, we were uncomfortable. Yet we must still sit there on our hard wooden forms long after the Queen had gone. What had been an honour to endure for the Queen had become only an imposition now that it was done at the behest of some unknown official.

We departed from the scene at last in grumbling and discontent, and not for an hour or so did the beauty and the grandeur of the unforgettable scene in the Abbey come uppermost in our minds again, so that we said, "It was worth it."

Throughout all those hours of the service the Queen had been superb. Only once did she falter from perfection, and that so slightly that few noticed her error. So well had she learned the service and so diligently had she rehearsed it that no single point escaped her.

10

Scotland, Ireland, Wales

BEFORE the Coronation there had been much talk of the Queen's winning the Derby of 1953 with her colt Aureole. This was the first year in which she could indulge her love for horse-racing to the full, and she was able to bring into use the knowledge of breeding and training which she had been acquiring since girlhood, when her love for horses had been stirred by a gallant race by one of her father's horses called Hypericum.

The Coronation Derby was run only four days after the Coronation itself, and there were many who doubted that the Queen would, after all, manage to be at Epsom to see her horse attempt to win the most important prize in racing. Her Majesty's engagement diary showed that June 1953 was one of the most crowded months of the Queen's life, there being seventy-six major engagements during the thirty days in addition to the Coronation itself.

Following the heavy strains of Coronation Day there were days crowded with work. The Queen and Prince Philip showed themselves five times on the famous Centre Balcony of Buckingham Palace on Coronation night. The floodlights had been switched on at 9.45 P.M., and when they were finally switched off at 11.30 it was a sign that there would be no more appearances.

During the evening the Queen had broadcast to the

whole world. "I have in sincerity pledged myself to your service, as so many of you are pledged to mine. Throughout all my life and with all my heart I shall strive to be worthy of your trust," she said; ". . . although my experience is so short and my task so new. . . .

"I have behind me, not only the splendid traditions and the annals of more than a thousand years, but the living strength and majesty of the Commonwealth and Empire. . . . I am sure that this, my Coronation, is not the symbol of a power and a splendour that are gone, but a declaration of our hopes for the future. . . . As this day draws to its close I know that my abiding memory of it will be, not only the solemnity and beauty of the ceremony, but the inspiration of your loyalty and affection."

By 10.30 next morning, June 3, the Queen was in the garden of the Palace presenting Coronation Medals to the 2400 members of contingents from the Commonwealth. An hour later she invested Sir David Maxwell Fyfe (now Lord Kilmuir) with the insignia of Knight Grand Cross of the Royal Victorian Order, and five minutes later bestowed a Knighthood in the same Order on the Right Hon. David Eccles, Minister of Works, who had been responsible for the street decorations, the stands, and the structural arrangements inside Westminster Abbey for the Coronation. After lunch the Queen drove with Prince Philip through a wide area of North-west London, and at 8.30 P.M. presided at a State Banquet in the Dining Room at the Palace and, in response to the cheering crowds, Her Majesty and His Royal Highness appeared on the balcony just before midnight.

June 4 was crowded with further audiences. At 11.50 A.M. the Queen received an officer and four Gurkhas who had been among the troops in the Coronation procession.

At noon the Queen saw Queen Salote of Tonga. Besides congratulating her on her stoicism in riding right round the Coronation route without once sheltering from the rain Queen Elizabeth took the opportunity of discussing her own forthcoming visit to Tonga during the Commonwealth tour planned to commence in November. At 12.10 P.M. Her Majesty saw the Sultan of Zanzibar, and at 12.20, with the Sultans of Johore, Selangor, Kelantan, Perak, Brunei, and Lahej present, she laughingly discussed with His Highness of Kelantan his wet ride with Queen Salote. At 2 P.M. the Queen, with Prince Philip, set out for the drive through North-west London. And at 8.30 P.M. a second State Banquet was held in the Dining Room of the Palace. Again they appeared on the balcony of the Palace in response to the demanding roar of the crowd.

Early after breakfast the following day the Queen and Prince Philip were riding the horses Winston and Yokefelt, which they were to ride at the Trooping the Colour ceremony on June 11. Then there was a visit from Prince Bertil of Sweden, who presented Queen Elizabeth with the Order of Seraphim, on behalf of the King of Sweden. At 11 A.M. the Queen received the envoys from overseas countries, including deputations from the Commonwealth. At 8 P.M. the Queen and Prince Philip attended a Lancaster House dinner given by Sir Winston Churchill, deputizing for the Foreign Minister, Mr Anthony Eden, who was ill. The guests included the Queen Mother, Princess Margaret, the Duke and Duchess of Gloucester, the Duchess of Kent, the Commonwealth Prime Ministers, and Mr Malik, the Russian Ambassador. At 10 P.M. Her Majesty gave a reception at Buckingham Palace. She appeared on the floodlit balcony at midnight to wave to a cheering crowd estimated at 60,000.

Sandringham holidays mean days of happy relaxation for the Queen. But each year there are such important engagements as presenting prizes to the pupils of West Newton Sunday School on the Sandringham Estate.

Prince Philip has always taken a keen interest in all things scientific, and he never misses an opportunity to further scientific education in Britain and elsewhere in the Commonwealth. Here he watches a chemistry experiment at Uppingham School.

The ‘korowai’ cloak is the hig
mark of esteem that the Maori
bestow, and here the Queen we
hers as she leaves a reception
Rotorua with the Minister
Maori Affairs, Mr Ernest Corb
during her tour of New Zeal
early in 1954.

The welcome of Fiji to the ro
travellers on their round-the-wo
tour of 1953–54 was as spectacu
as any they received. At ni
grass-skirted torchbearers esco
the royal car through the darke
streets of Suva to a State ball in
Grand Pacific Hotel.

Despite the crush of engagements, the Queen was obviously in the best of health when she arrived on Epsom Downs for the Derby. As usual, she went into the saddling enclosure. She saw Aureole and talked to W. H. Carr, his jockey, and Captain Charles Moore, her racing manager, and Aureole's trainer, Captain Cecil Boyd-Rochfort.

Aureole, son of Hyperion out of King George VI's mare Angelola, was foaled at the Hampton Court stud, and the Queen, as Princess Elizabeth, had fed him with a milk-bottle within a few days of his birth. Seeing Gordon Richards standing with Pinza, the horse he was to ride, and which was joint favourite with Aureole, Her Majesty told the jockey and Mr Norman Bertie, Pinza's trainer, that she thought Aureole would have to watch not only Pinza but the French colt Pink Horse, which had a good chance.

The leaders of the race in the order of their finishing were: Pinza, Aureole, and Pink Horse.

Between the Derby and Royal Ascot in 1953 there were only ten days. But into these ten days the Queen managed to cram as wide a variety of engagements as any sovereign in history. On June 8, with Prince Philip, the Queen Mother, and Princess Margaret, she attended a gala performance in the Royal Opera House after an afternoon drive with her husband through South-east London. On June 9 the Queen and Prince Philip attended a service of thanksgiving in St Paul's Cathedral, and in the afternoon drove through South-west London. In the evening they attended a Government Evening Reception and a dinner party given by the Prime Minister to the Commonwealth Prime Ministers. After dinner talk turned to the forthcoming tour of the Commonwealth and the sights and experiences the royal travellers would enjoy.

Engagements for June 10 included a visit at 2.20 P.M. to the Royal Tournament at Earls Court and the Queen's weekly audience for the Prime Minister at 6.30 P.M. On June 11 Her Majesty, mounted on famous police horse Winston, again took the salute at the ceremony of Trooping the Colour on Horse Guards, and an immense crowd saw her lead her Guards back to the Palace. Afterwards, from the Centre Balcony of the Palace, the Royal Family watched the fly-past of the Royal Air Force. At 6.50 P.M. the Queen and Prince Philip attended a cocktail party given by the Grenadier Guards in Chelsea.

There was a City lunch at the Guildhall on June 12 and another evening reception at Buckingham Palace. But before setting out for her lunch in the City the Queen saw U.S. General Matthew Ridgway, Supreme Allied Commander, Europe, when he came to say farewell. At the Guildhall Her Majesty invested the Lord Mayor of London, Sir Rupert De la Bère, with the insignia of Knight Commander of the Royal Victorian Order.

The Court went into residence at Windsor Castle on June 13, when the Queen and Prince Philip also paid an official visit to the Royal Borough of Windsor and Eton. But next morning Her Majesty and the Prince boarded H.M.S. *Surprise* at Portsmouth for the Royal Review of the Fleet. *Surprise* sailed down the lines of ships, 330 ships of the Royal and Merchant Navies and ships from navies of other countries.

Royal Ascot opened on June 16. The Queen and Prince Philip attended all four days. If Her Majesty had her disappointments during that racing season she also had her triumphs, for her horse Choir Boy, ridden by Doug Smith, won the Royal Hunt Cup on June 17. At the second Ascot meeting, on July 18, Aureole again had his chance against Pinza in the King George VI and Queen Elizabeth Stakes and was again beaten.

There were many knowledgeable racing men who wrote off this colt of the Queen's after that second defeat. Her Majesty, however, was confident that he could be a great horse, and her opinion always carries weight with those who know their breeding and training. The Queen has an encyclopædic knowledge of pedigrees and breeding records. In her study is a book which contains the pedigrees of 45,000 racehorses and her racing ledger, which she keeps up herself. Into it go the records of all her horses. Her trainers send her these records at the end of every meeting. At the start of the season Her Majesty sets out her plans, and these cover the whole flat-racing season. The Queen also plans the breeding policy for her brood mares and stallions, deciding the mating and selecting the races for the horses in training.

On June 22 the Queen gave lunch to the Right Hon. Vincent Massey, Governor-General of Canada, and that evening, after her weekly audience for the Prime Minister, she set out with Prince Philip for the Coronation visit to Scotland.

This was almost in the nature of a second Coronation. The Queen received the keys of the City of Edinburgh on June 23 before driving in state to the Palace of Holyroodhouse. The royal couple lunched with the Corporation of Edinburgh, and in the evening held a Presentation Party in Holyroodhouse.

Next day Her Majesty, with Prince Philip, preceded by the Honours of Scotland (Scottish Regalia), drove in state to St Giles's Cathedral to attend a National Service. The day before, on their arrival in the Scottish capital, the Queen and Prince Philip had driven unexpectedly to the

Cathedral to inspect the new royal chairs which had been installed there and to rehearse also the ceremony.

The date is significant in Scottish history. On June 24, 1314, Robert Bruce, greatest of the Scottish kings, defeated the English at Bannockburn, and thus struck a decisive blow for Scottish freedom. Queen Elizabeth, realizing that her Scottish Coronation visit would coincide with the anniversary of the battle, had herself asked that the National Service should be held in St Giles's. It was a gesture which delighted all Scotsmen.

On the day the Honours of Scotland were borne in two carriages which led the royal procession. The carriages and the royal coach were each flanked on either side by five Royal Archers of the Queen's Body Guard for Scotland. In the coach nearest the Queen was the Crown, borne by the Duke of Hamilton and Brandon. In the leading carriages the Lord High Constable, the Earl of Home, bore the Sword, and Lord Crawford and Balcarres, as Premier Earl of Scotland, carried the Sceptre. Ahead the Royal Banner of the Kings of Scots fluttered in the breeze in the hands of Lord Dundee, who was on horseback and supported by two Squires to the Banner. St Andrew's flag was carried farther ahead by the Master of Lauderdale, on behalf of his brother, Lord Lauderdale, Hereditary Bearer of the flag.

As the Queen and Prince Philip got down from their coach at the great West Door of the Cathedral the trumpets rang out. The service opened with the text on which Edinburgh founded its motto—*Nisi Dominus frustra* ("Except the Lord build the house, they labour in vain that build it")—and the congregation responded, "Except the Lord keep the city, the watchman waketh but in vain."

Then followed Psalm xx, "We will rejoice in thy salvation, and in the name of our God we will set up our banners," which had been sung at Scone in 1651 at the coronation of Charles II, and Psalm lxxxiv, "Behold, O God our shield, and look upon the face of Thine anointed," which had been sung at the coronation of Charles I at Holyrood in 1633. The prayer for the Queen besought God to "exalt her that she may hold the sceptre of salvation; enrich her with such gifts of Thy mercy as shall bring her holiness, and grant unto her by Thine inspiration even so to rule her people in meekness and humility, as Thou didst cause Solomon to obtain a kingdom of peace."

The Lord Lyon and the Dean of the Chapel Royal conducted the Queen and Prince Philip to the sanctuary. The Queen stood alone by the Holy Table, and the Dean said, "We the members of this Scottish congregation here assembled greet your Majesty, our crowned and anointed Sovereign Lady. . . . We pledge anew ourselves and all that we have to the service of our Queen and country; and, as we wish God to be merciful to us, shall always be to your Majesty true and faithful."

Raising his hand, the Dean blessed the Queen in the words, "The Lord bless and keep thee, and as He has made thee Queen over His people, so may He still prosper thee in this world, and in the world to come make thee partaker of His everlasting felicity."

Queen Elizabeth handed the Honours of Scotland one by one to their bearers as they knelt before her to receive them. The Queen and Prince Philip went out from the greyness of the Cathedral into sunshine and into the warmth of a greeting from the massed thousands outside that had rarely been matched on any occasion of their lives.

In the afternoon the Queen and Prince Philip attended a

garden party in the grounds of Holyroodhouse, during which Her Majesty awarded Coronation honours. The following day was again filled with engagements. There were visits to Paisley and Glasgow, and lunch with the Corporation of Glasgow, followed by a Review of Youth at Hampden Park. June 26 engagements included the presentation of new colours to the 1st Battalion, Argyll and Sutherland Highlanders, the opening of a new door and planting of a tree at Canongate Kirk, Edinburgh, by Prince Philip, and an evening reception by the Queen and the Prince at Holyroodhouse.

A State drive to receive the keys of Edinburgh Castle, a visit to a display at Murrayfield, attendance at a gala performance of the *Masque of Edinburgh*, and a fireworks display in Queen's Park was the programme for June 27, and on the following day Queen Elizabeth installed her husband as a Knight of the Thistle and later attended Divine Service in St Giles's Cathedral. June 29 was spent in visiting Lanark, Hamilton, Motherwell, Airdrie, and Coatbridge. That night, the Scottish visit over, the Queen and Prince Philip boarded the train for London.

Their Coronation visit to Scotland had been a triumph and a heart-warming experience. There had been fears in some quarters that some misguided enthusiast for the cause of Scottish nationalism might try to achieve publicity. The Queen had shown her attitude to Scots and Scotland by the selection of Robert Bruce's day for the National Service. All Scotland accepted the fact that a direct descendant of Robert Bruce had come among them and had followed the Honours of Scotland to the High Table as had the Scottish sovereigns of old.

But there was one cause for disturbance in Scottish minds. The rumour had been spreading for some months that Queen Elizabeth had decided to give up Balmoral Castle as her Scottish residence. Not private enough, the rumour had it. The house is too old and too cold, said the knowing ones. In fact, the rumours arose from inquiries that had been made by Queen Elizabeth the Queen Mother which finally resulted in her buying the Castle of Mey, in the far north of Scotland. At no time did the Queen consider disposing of Balmoral.

Within two hours of her return to Buckingham Palace from Euston the Queen held an investiture while Prince Philip looked in at the Test Match at Lord's, where England were playing Australia. At 2.15 P.M. Queen Elizabeth and Prince Philip saw the Queen Mother and Princess Margaret off to Southern Rhodesia from London Airport. The royal travellers were attending the Rhodes Centenary Exhibition at Bulawayo. By 3 P.M. Prince Philip was at Wimbledon watching the tennis.

July 1 marked the setting out of the Queen for a visit to Northern Ireland. But before leaving London Airport with Prince Philip there was the ordinary business of the day to complete, correspondence to answer, and papers to sign. And at noon the Queen knighted Major-General Gascoigne, who had commanded the Coronation troops, and invested him with the insignia of Knight Commander of the Royal Victorian Order. At 12.30 she saw the Home Secretary, the Right Hon. James Chuter Ede, Sir Ian Fraser, M.P., and Mr Benjamin Britten, the composer. Then off to London Airport to take plane to Aldergrove.

Throughout July the Queen kept engagements which identified her with a wide cross-section of the national life. With Prince Philip she attended a review of ex-Servicemen and women in Hyde Park; attended a ball at Hurlingham organized by the Royal Empire Society and the Victoria

League and the Over-Seas League; inspected the Royal Canadian Mounted Police detachment which had attended the Coronation. Twice during the month the Queen presented the badge of the Order of Merit—to Dr Wilder Penfield, Director of the Montreal Neurological Institute and Professor of Neurology and Neurosurgery at McGill University; and to Mr Walter de la Mare, the poet and story-writer. There was a private investiture for the Knight Grand Cross of the Royal Victorian Order for the Marquess of Cholmondeley.

On July 7 the Queen received Lord Salisbury, the acting Foreign Secretary, to lunch at the Palace and heard about his proposed visit to Washington, where the policy towards Russia, German reunification, and European defence were to be discussed.

On July 8 the Queen and Prince Philip left London for their Coronation tour of Wales—to Cardiff, the Rhondda Valley, Hirwain, Swansea, Llanelly, Caernarvon, where the ceremony of surrendering the key was held at the castle. The one disappointment to the ordinary people was the fact that Her Majesty did not name Prince Charles as Prince of Wales, as it had been rumoured that, without any justification other than fervent Welsh desire, she would do. Other stops on the Welsh trip were at Rhyl, Wrexham, and Llangollen, where the royal visitors attended the International Eisteddfod and where the Queen saw the slab of blue pennant stone which marks the spot on the railway station where she first set foot in Wales after her accession.

The Queen was back in London by July 11 in time to drive to Sandown Park for the races on that day.

On July 15 the Queen with Prince Philip reviewed the Royal Air Force at Odiham, Hampshire. Next day she received the 1953 Mount Everest Expedition members and knighted Colonel John Hunt, the leader, and awarded Mr Edmund Hillary, the New Zealander who had reached the top with Sherpa Tenzing, a knighthood of the Order of the British Empire. Sherpa Tenzing Norkay received the George Medal. On the same day at 3 P.M. the Queen held a Presentation Party for overseas debutantes.

On July 21 Lord Salisbury reported the results of his Washington talks.

The great Royal River Pageant took place on July 22, and in the evening the Queen and Prince Philip were present at the International Horse Show at the White City. On July 27 there was a welcome visitor at Buckingham Palace in the person of Mrs Franklin Roosevelt. On the following day it was racing again at Goodwood, with the Queen and Prince Philip staying again at Arundel Castle, and on July 31 at 11.30 A.M. a Privy Council meeting was held at Goodwood. On August 1 a further Privy Council meeting was held at Buckingham Palace.

Her Majesty went into residence at Balmoral in August as usual, and, as usual, broke her holiday in Scotland to travel to Doncaster for the St Leger. On this occasion she took the Prime Minister and Lady Churchill back with her for a week-end at the Castle and long reminiscences of the months that had passed and discussions on the crowded days that lay ahead.

By now the Queen was deep in her preparations for the round-the-world trip that she would make on her Commonwealth tour. There were literally hundreds of frocks and gowns to be selected, and Mr Norman Hartnell had now a regular weekly audience at which he submitted his designs and discussed materials suitable for the extraordinary diversity of climates that the Queen would experience on her trip.

Back in London on October 14 the Queen immediately began a series of meetings with the representatives of the Commonwealth countries she would visit on her trip. General Sir Dallas Brooks, Governor of Victoria, was received at the Palace on October 15, and on October 19 the Queen and Prince Philip had tea with Sir Thomas White, High Commissioner for Australia, and Lady White at Stoke Lodge. On October 26 the Queen and her husband had tea with the High Commissioner for Ceylon and Lady Wijeyeratne, and on November 3 went to tea with the High Commissioner for New Zealand and Lady Doidge. Next day Her Majesty received the Earl of Ranfurly, Governor and Commander-in-Chief of the Bahamas.

There were many other important engagements in between. On October 17 the Queen unveiled the Commonwealth Air Force Memorial at Runnymede. On October 29 Her Majesty held an evening Presentation Party at Buckingham Palace for members of the Diplomatic Corps. The Queen opened another session of Parliament on November 3, and on November 6 received General Gruenther, Supreme Allied Commander Europe, and Mrs Gruenther in audience at the Palace. On November 18 the Governor-General of Pakistan came to the Palace.

The departure for the West Indies on the first stage of the Commonwealth tour was now imminent. *Gothic*, the Shaw Savill ship chosen as the royal yacht for the sea stages of the trip, sailed from King George V Docks on November 10. On November 20 the Queen received a present of two polo ponies from President Peron, of the Argentine, at the hands of the Argentine Ambassador to London, and later that day gave a sherry party to the members of the British Government—her last official engagement before she left with Prince Philip for Newfoundland and Bermuda.

She had exactly two clear days to settle all the final details of a trip which would take her round the world. Before leaving London Airport at 9.02 P.M. on November 23 she saw the Lord Chamberlain, who presented an address from the House of Lords, and the Vice-Chamberlain, who presented a similar address from the House of Commons. Her Majesty invested Lieutenant-Colonel Sir Piers Legh, Master of her Household, with the insignia of Knight Commander of the Order of the Bath, and she was then ready to say her last good-byes to her children and to get ready for the drive to the airport. It was that kind of departure day.

In Coronation year Queen Elizabeth II carried out 452 separate public engagements.

11

Bonds of Commonwealth

"It may well be that the journey the Queen is about to take will be no less auspicious, and the treasure she brings back no less bright, than when Drake first sailed an English ship around the world," said Winston Churchill in the House of Commons on November 19, 1953, in a reference to the round-the-world tour the Queen and Prince Philip would begin when they left London Airport on November 23 for the first stages of their flight to Bermuda.

There could never have been a more heart-warming send-off for any British sovereign. For thirteen miles along the route from Buckingham Palace to London Airport the pavements were lined with cheering people despite the cold and the damp of the chilly evening. When *Canopus*, the B.O.A.C. aircraft which was to take the Queen and Prince Philip across the Atlantic, took off into the darkness the roar of its engines was almost drowned by the noise of cheering.

The Queen made history on this flight. She was the first sovereign ever to fly across the Atlantic.

When *Canopus* landed at Gander, almost ten hours after leaving London Airport, there were 200 Canadians who had been there most of the night waiting to chant, "We want the Queen," and to sing, "For she's a jolly good fellow." The Queen and Prince Philip appeared at the doorway of the aeroplane just before it took off again from Gander.

"I am so pleased to be back in Canada, even though it is for such a very short stay," Her Majesty told Commissioner M. F. E. Anthony, of the Royal Canadian Mounted Police, who had mounted guard on the plane during its stop. The Queen recognized among the guard Corporal E. S. Hunt, a Mountie who had accompanied Commissioner Anthony on the royal tour in 1951, and shook him warmly by the hand.

It was 9.55 A.M. local time when *Canopus* landed at Kindley Bay airfield, Bermuda. In a setting of brilliant poinsettias, hibiscus, and palms the royal visitors were greeted by Lieutenant-General Sir Alexander Hood, Governor of Bermuda. "The first seed of the plant which grew in Britain fell here in Bermuda, and the climate and soil seem to have suited it," said the Queen in her reply to an address of welcome. "I am happy to-day to be able to visit this first of my Parliaments Overseas and to find so fine and vigorous a growth."

A crowded day included meeting thousands of children and ex-Servicemen at the Royal Bermuda Yacht Club, a tour through Great Sound to Mangrove Bay, in the western part of the island, in the converted ferry-boat *Wilhelmina*, and a visit to King Edward VII Memorial Hospital at Paget.

After a garden party in the grounds of Government House, attended by 1200 guests, the Queen and Prince Philip dined informally at Government House with thirty of the island's leading citizens, and retired early. Through her open window Her Majesty could hear the night-long song of the Bermudian tree-frogs as she rested.

It was still dark when the royal travellers were about again, to prepare for the flight from Bermuda to Jamaica, but already the crowds were gathering outside Government House to bid them farewell. They left behind them a growing storm of controversy over an alleged case of colour discrimination at the dinner party the night before.

The Queen could not have been unaware for many months past of the possibility that difficult situations might arise during a 50,000-mile tour spread over six months and taking in fifteen countries. In Bermuda Her Majesty had been gracious and friendly to all she had met. But on November 27, after the royal visitors had left for Jamaica, Mr E. T. Richards, a coloured lawyer, raising the matter of the absence of any coloured person at the Queen's welcome dinner, described it as "the biggest slip made in Bermuda this century." Mr Richards said that it would be unfortunate if there should be repercussions after such a glorious visit.

How swiftly any slight doubts there might have existed regarding the Queen's own views on the subject were dispelled in Jamaica! From the first moment of her arrival Her Majesty made it plain that questions of colour had no place in her thoughts.

The islanders greeted the Queen with even greater fervour than had the people of Bermuda. This was the first time any British sovereign had visited the island, and the people in the villages and towns in the enthusiasm of their greeting echoed the words of the welcoming speech made at the airport of Montego Bay by the Hon. H. E. Lake, of Antigua: "This joyful event gives a new meaning of urgency to our determination that our territories should stand ever closer together, drawing the same inspiration and working for the same ideals within the great family of free peoples which owes allegiance to Your Majesty."

At Discovery Bay, Falmouth, St Ann's Bay, and Spanish Town, on the way to Kingston, the capital, the royal car stopped so that the Queen could receive addresses of welcome and the cheers of big crowds. The onlookers were delighted with the way in which Queen Elizabeth acknowledged the cheers and the flag-waving, missing no one with her smiles. The women were quick to notice that, despite the severe and humid heat of midday, in which few ever drive in open cars, the Queen and the Prince travelled with the hood down. Her Majesty, though she sheltered under a parasol on the clear parts of the road, always laid it aside the moment she saw people waiting to greet her.

There were many comments on Prince Philip's infectious laughter and the readiness he showed to share a joke with the townspeople he met at each stop.

In intense tropical heat in the Legislative Council Chamber in Kingston Queen Elizabeth addressed all the members of the Legislative except Mr Norman Manley (then leader of the Opposition), who was ill with heart-strain. The Queen said: "In the wider sphere of world affairs the British Commonwealth and Empire have shown to the world that the strongest bonds of all are those which are recorded, not in documents, but in the hearts of the people who share the same beliefs and the same aims. Here in this region you are showing that you are bound together in the same way by common economic interests and common political purposes. Those ties are powerful, but not so strong as the bonds of human friendship and the unity which comes from sharing the same heritage and aspirations and the same loyalty."

This speech made a very marked impression on all Jamaicans.

Three thousand Jamaicans from all sections of the community came to Government House that evening for a party in the garden, where the bougainvillea bushes were floodlit. The Queen and Prince Philip walked among the guests and talked with many hundreds of them. Mixed choirs sang Jamaican folk-songs, and there was also a Jamaican ballet.

But next day the Queen and Prince Philip were again reminded of what unexpected events a royal progress such as theirs could produce. As they walked towards the wharf on November 27 to embark in *Gothic* for the voyage to Panama, middle-aged Warren Kidd, a Jamaican schoolmaster, ducked under the ropes, evaded the police, and spread his linen jacket in the roadway in front of the Queen. Her Majesty smiled as the coloured schoolmaster went down on his knees to her, but the man was hustled away and charged under the Lunacy Laws—an act which caused considerable indignation among the coloured people of the city. Their annoyance was only partially relieved by the release of Warren Kidd. It took a letter from seven British M.P.'s addressed to Kidd with the words, "We are sorry that for the moment your generous intentions were misunderstood. We should like to thank you on behalf of many British citizens for your courteous actions," to assuage the hurt feelings of Kidd and his friends.

Her Majesty dealt with her Jamaican subjects in a manner rather different from that of some officials. It had been arranged that the Chief of the Maroons (Negroes) should receive an audience of the Queen, but a mix-up in messages resulted in the Chief's missing the appointment. The Chief's envoy sought an audience on November 26,

Australia's children gave the Queen and Prince Philip an overwhelming welcome at every stop on the long tour of the Dominion in 1954. A great crowd of youngsters, estimated at more than 110,000, cheered the royal travellers as they passed through their ranks in a specially equipped car at Sydney's Showground.

Days packed with crowded and often exhausting engagements still failed to dim the radiant picture that Her Majesty the Queen presented on all occasions of her Commonwealth tour of 1953–54. Here Her Majesty is seen arriving at a civic reception and dinner given by the New South Wales Government in Sydney.

One of the most touching moments of the Queen's reign was when John Aguh, a blind leper in Eastern Nigeria, told her during her tour there in February 1956, "We cannot express enough our joy and happiness at seeing you here."

A rare picture of a dubbing. Here Queen Elizabeth II knights Air Marshal Claude Pelly, C.-in-C., Middle East Air Forces, during her brief stay in Aden while returning from her tour of New Zealand, Australia, and Ceylon in 1954.

(*By courtesy of the Air Ministry*)

but there was no chance to fit one into the crowded programme. The Queen consented to meet the Chief at 10.30 on November 27, but the envoy had returned to Maroon Town. Her Majesty thereupon delayed the audience until 11 A.M., but the Chief had not arrived by the time *Gothic* had to sail. On her way to the wharf the Queen acceded to the request of one of the local newspapers to pose for a photograph with all the representatives of the West Indian Parliaments present.

"The Queen captured the Isthmus of Panama single-handed," one commentator said in describing the extraordinary scene of enthusiasm for the royal visitors as *Gothic* passed through the Panama Canal into the Pacific Ocean. Ahead lay the long run south-westward to Fiji.

It was December 17 when the Queen and Prince Philip reached Suva Bay, in the Fiji Islands. Her Majesty was the first sovereign to visit the islands since they were ceded to Britain in 1874. *Gothic* steamed in through the long coral reefs, and the Governor, Sir Ronald Garvey, and Lady Garvey came aboard at 9 A.M. with the *matanivuana*, the Fijian master of ceremonies. Five chiefs from the island of Mbau and the province of Rewa, all wearing Fijian bark-cloth dresses, followed them, and the Queen and Prince Philip received the *cuvuikelekele*, the invitation to land. Four chiefs squatted on deck, and one advanced on his knees to offer the Queen a *tabua* (whale's tooth), traditionally the most prized Fijian possession.

That this was no normal occasion was shown when the royal visitors landed. It is a tradition of Fiji that important guests shall be greeted in silence. Silence greeted the Queen and Prince Philip for just one brief moment as they stepped ashore, and then a great roar of applause rang out. Then, as if they had been shocked by this break in tradition, the people fell silent all along the way to Albert Park, where the royal couple drank the traditional drink of *kava* (made from the roots of the yangonna-tree) to the triumphant shout of "Maca" ("It is finished") as they put down their coconut-shell cups after drinking. At night, when they attended a State ball, 200 torchbearers ran beside their car through the darkness, and later, when the Queen and Prince Philip appeared on the hotel balcony, a choir of many hundreds among a crowd of 10,000 sang the national anthem and the Hallelujah Chorus before ending with the Fijian song of farewell, "Isa Lei."

When she addressed the Legislative Council the Queen referred to the benefits that the inter-racial unity of Fiji—Fijians, Indians, Chinese, and Europeans—had brought to the islands. But she was fully alive to the possible causes of dissension in the future when the Fijians, with major ownership of the land, would be in a numerical minority to the Indian population.

The Queen's visit brought to Fiji thousands of her subjects from all parts of the Pacific. Among them was John Christian, a direct descendant of Fletcher Christian of the mutiny of the *Bounty*, and his wife, who had come from Pitcairn Island, about 3500 miles away. An aged chief came more than 200 miles despite advice that the journey might be dangerous for him. "I know only two rulers—God and the Queen," he protested. "I may see the one when I die, but I intend to see the other while I live."

From Fiji the Queen and Prince Philip flew to Tonga on December 19 to a welcome from Queen Salote and her people that made the Queen exclaim, "No wonder these are called the Friendly Isles." To greet them also was a London taxicab which Salote had ordered after riding in one during her visit to Britain for the Coronation.

The following dawn, when they set out for New Zealand, the royal travellers were wakened by the soft music of the Tongan nose-flutes played by four musicians beneath their windows in the white-walled Palace of Nukualofa. In the background was the constant surge of the surf on the reef and on the white sands of the beach, and the night sky was lit by flaming fibre torches held by the 400 Tongan guards.

As the royal barge left to take the Queen and Prince Philip back to *Gothic* the royal travellers were garlanded with flowers. A Tongan band played "Rule, Britannia!" again and again as *Gothic* got under way, and friendly Tongans cast *leis* (flower garlands) in her path.

And so to New Zealand and more great scenes of enthusiasm. The Queen stepped ashore in Auckland on December 23 into a persistent drizzle of rain that matched her Coronation Day. Yet she acted throughout the day as if the sun that she had known in Tonga and Fiji was still beating down on her. When the drenched crowd outside the Town Hall shouted, "Give her an umbrella," Mr K. N. Buttle, Auckland's deputy Mayor, handed to Mr S. G. Holland, the Prime Minister, a plastic raincoat. The crowd cheered, and the Queen said to Mr Buttle, "Thank you," bowed, and added after a pause, "Sir Walter Raleigh."

Her Majesty, rising to reply to the speech of welcome, shrugged the raincoat from her shoulders and stood unprotected again in the rain, a gesture that brought renewed storms of cheering. "This is the first time I have spoken to New Zealanders in their own homeland," the Queen said. "Can you wonder then that I am proud to be here and that I am looking forward with hope and happiness to the journey I am to take with my husband from this city to the southernmost parts of South Island?"

Queen Elizabeth was the first reigning monarch to visit New Zealand. Her progress through the two islands was a mounting triumph. From Auckland on Christmas Day Her Majesty broadcast to the whole Commonwealth the traditional royal Christmas message, "I want to show that the Crown is not merely an abstract symbol of our unity, but a personal and living bond between you and me," she said.

There were memorable incidents at many places on the tour. At Eden Terrace sixty King's Empire Veterans waited by the roadside to see the royal car go by, and Mr L. G. Eayre, of the Duke of Edinburgh's Own Volunteer Rifles, almost blind, excitedly waved his white stick. "I saw them," he cried. At Henderson a floral carpet in which had been worked the words "Welcome to Henderson" covered the road for thirty-two feet. The Maoris at a *powhiri* (dance of welcome) at Waitangi—where on February 6, 1840, the Maori chiefs signed over the sovereignty of their country to Queen Victoria—made the Queen "God of the Sea" and Prince Philip "God of War." Mr Hone Rankin, a Maori magistrate, speaking in his own tongue, said, "Welcome to greatness, to sanctity and exalted Majesty. We thank God for a century and more of British rule."

As the royal progress moved southward memories piled on memories. Three lambs, their coats dyed respectively red, white, and blue, greeted the visitors at Tuakau; at Ngaruawahia King Koroki, chief of the Waikatos, a tribe which had refused to acknowledge the Waitangi treaty, was visited by the Queen and Prince Philip, and green-painted war canoes, each manned by sixty men, raced along the river; the royal travellers visited the Glow-worm Grotto on the Black River, where hundreds of thousands of glow-worms shine like stars in the blackness of the cavern roof.

The ceremony at Rotorua when the Queen and Prince Philip were created Paramount Chiefs before the representatives of every Maori tribe; the State opening of the thirtieth Parliament in the Old Chambers of the Upper House, in Wellington, on January 12; the Privy Council meeting on the following day, which was the first ever to be held in New Zealand—these were other highlights of a tour which, in the words of Mr Holland, had released "such a flood of loyalty from all parts of the Commonwealth as had never been surpassed in all its history."

On January 30, 1954, the moment for parting came. The waiting crowds at the wharf at Bluff sang "Now is the hour" as the Queen and Prince Philip prepared to board *Gothic* again. "It is impossible to calculate the benefits of this remarkable tour," said Mr Holland. "New Zealand has known nothing like it before."

"We have enjoyed every minute of our stay," said the Queen.

Sydney's welcome to the royal travellers when they landed on February 3 surpassed in noise and excitement anything which had gone before. More than a million people were in the crowds to greet the Queen and her husband. "The Queen of Australia comes home at last," cried one commentator as Her Majesty stepped ashore, and it was with that sentiment that the people cheered so loudly that the address of welcome was drowned. But as the Queen stepped to the microphone absolute silence fell on the crowd, and Her Majesty's words were heard clearly everywhere. "I have always looked forward to my first visit to this country, but now there is the added satisfaction to me that I am able to meet my Australian people as their Queen. . . . I am proud indeed to be at the head of a nation that has achieved so much," she said.

Throughout the long tour that took the Queen and Prince Philip as far north as Cairns, in the Great Barrier Reef, and as far west as Perth, in Western Australia, it was once more memorable scenes and unforgettable incidents all the way. On the trip from Sydney to Newcastle one man called, "Hurry back, dear; we shall miss you," and was rewarded by a special smile from the Queen. At Newcastle at the Broken Hill Proprietary Steelworks ten men who were presented had removed the callouses from their hands with emery paper. Joe Sleishman, sixty-seven-year-old oven worker came to work in his best suit, and when told to put on his working clothes compromised by wearing his working shirt with his best trousers.

At Bathurst sixteen-year-old Jill Forrest read a speech of welcome in which she said, "We all hope that as we grow older we may follow your gracious example and give you and our fellow-countrymen the devoted and selfless service you yourself have promised and already given," and that summed up the feelings of all Australians for their Queen.

Her Majesty wore her Coronation gown for the opening of the Federal Parliament in Canberra on February 15. "You are here as my colleagues, my friends and advisers," the Queen told the statesmen and politicians. At the State Banquet on February 16 Mr Robert Menzies, the Australian Prime Minister, in a moving speech, told Her Majesty, "You are in your own country, among your own people . . . we are yours, all parties, all creeds. Skilled as you are in the noble arts of Queenship, young though you are in years, may I say this to you: 'You may count on us.' "

Tasmania, Victoria, Queensland the great Outback, South Australia, and Western Australia—all of them provided new and exciting experiences, until on April 1 the Queen broadcast a farewell message from her sitting-room in *Gothic* as the ship steamed out into the Indian Ocean: "I want to say to you, my Australian people, how sad we are to be leaving the shores of your wonderful land. This visit has been most interesting and enjoyable to me, but I hope that it has also served to remind you of the wonderful heritage which we share, and I hope it has demonstrated that the Crown is a human link between all peoples who owe allegiance to me—an allegiance of mutual love and respect and never of compulsion. . . ."

Gothic reached the Cocos-Keeling group of islands in the Indian Ocean on April 5, and took the Queen and Prince Philip on to Ceylon on April 10. On April 19 at Kandy, the old capital of the Sinhalese kings, the royal couple watched a *raja perahera* (royal procession) at the Buddhist Temple of the Tooth.

Aden; then by air to Entebbe, Uganda, and the Owen Falls Dam; Tobruk, where the Queen and Prince Philip had their reunion with Prince Charles and Princess Anne, who had come there in the royal yacht *Britannia*—Malta and Gibraltar brought the great round-the-world tour almost to an end. Now all that remained was the run home along the coastlines of Spain and Portugal, through the Bay of Biscay, and into the Port of London.

On May 15, 173 days after they had left London, the Queen and Prince Philip were home again. The citizens of London cheered them all the way from Westminster to Buckingham Palace, and a great crowd was waiting outside the Palace for the Royal Family to make the usual appearance on the Centre Balcony. The cheers were the expression of joy at their homecoming and congratulations for a job well done.

Throughout the tour Queen Elizabeth and Prince Philip had maintained an almost incredible resilience to strain—day after day of often tedious official functions, few days of rest, and none of complete rest except when on board ship They had met and overcome awkward situations—such as the open quarrel between the Western Australian Government and the Federal Government over the changes to the royal tour of Western Australia on account of a polio epidemic. (Such terms as "unnecessary and high-handed interference" had been used.) They had made millions of new loyalists and thousands of new friends. They had given to hundreds of outlying parts of the Commonwealth a new appreciation of what the Family of Nations means.

12

Dividing the List

QUEEN ELIZABETH and Prince Philip returned to London on May 15, 1954. Two free days followed, and on May 18 the first official business was a two-hour meeting of the Prince's Council of the Duchy of Cornwall, over which Her Majesty presided. On the same day the Queen saw Dr Jeronimo Remorino, the Argentine Foreign Minister, and Dr Alfredo Morales, Minister for Economic Affairs in Peron's Government, in London on a trade mission. At 2.45 P.M. the Queen received Sir David Eccles, Minister of Works, who reported on the work that had been carried out at Buckingham Palace while the Queen and Prince Philip had been circling the world.

On the evening of Monday, May 17, Her Majesty and the Duke of Edinburgh entertained the Cabinet Ministers to a sherry party at the Palace. The Opposition leaders, Mr Clement Attlee and Mr Clement Davies, were also present, and Mr Herbert Morrison. This was the first opportunity that Government leaders had had to express their congratulations on the success of the great trip. It was to be followed on May 19 by loyal addresses from both Houses of Parliament.

Now, already, the full force of official business had started again. Between May 18 and the end of 1954 the

Queen and Prince Philip carried out exactly 300 public engagements in Britain. But in that period Prince Philip also visited France and Germany from June 21 until June 27; Cowes and Dartmouth in the royal yacht *Britannia* from July 9 until July 12; and Canada from July 28 until August 23.

The pattern of the working life of Her Majesty and Prince Philip was now becoming clearer. Of the 300 engagements in the last seven months of 1954 only 33 were dual engagements for the Queen and her husband. For the rest of the time, so diverse and so widespread were the calls on their time, Her Majesty and Prince Philip had no alternative but to divide the list, even more than usual. That meant many days of separate activity as well as a year of work such as no sovereign and her consort had ever before attempted to carry through.

On May 19 the royal couple were entertained to luncheon by the Lord Mayor and Corporation of the City of London. Before the State drive through the crowded streets there was a pleasing little ceremony at the Palace when the wardens and clerk of the Worshipful Company of Gardeners presented Her Majesty with the bouquet which she carried on her drive.

The following day the Royal Family, including Prince Charles and Princess Anne, travelled north for an eleven-day stay at Balmoral.

On May 28 Prince Philip flew south to Cowdray Park for polo. On June 1 the Queen welcomed at a sherry party at the Palace the members of the French delegation visiting London for the fiftieth anniversary of the Entente Cordiale. Prince Philip, the Queen, Mother, and Princess Margaret were also present. Her Majesty talked with M. Le Troquer, President of the French National Assembly, M.

Corbin, President of the Anglo-French Society in Paris, and General Corniglion-Molinier. They recalled that in May 1908 in Buckingham Palace the Queen's great-grandfather, King Edward VII, when asked what he would say in his speech of welcome to M. Armand Fallières, the French President, replied, "I shall allude to *entente cordiale*." The speech that the King made at the State Banquet which followed has always been regarded as one of the most important ever made in the cause of Anglo-French understanding and co-operation.

Queen Elizabeth and Prince Philip were at Epsom for the Derby meeting on June 2, and also for the Oaks on June 4. There Aureole lived up to his name and started a golden year for the Queen by winning the Coronation Cup over the Derby course. On June 8 the Queen's engagements included receiving the new Indonesian Ambassador, audiences for Sir John Lomax, H.M. Ambassador to La Paz, Bolivia, and Sir Victor Mallet on his retirement from the Foreign Service, an audience for the Prime Minister, and a private visit to the Antique Dealers' Fair at Grosvenor House (a visit that she rarely misses). For Prince Philip the day included installation as Master of the Honourable Company of Master Mariners aboard H.M.S. *Wellington* by the Thames Embankment, and presiding at an English-Speaking Union dinner to General Gruenther, the Commander of the N.A.T.O. forces.

June 10 was Trooping the Colour day for the Queen, and on Winston she took the salute as the 1st Battalion Coldstream Guards trooped the colour on Horse Guards Parade. Prince Philip, whose thirty-third birthday it was, was with Her Majesty and watched with her from the Centre Balcony of the Palace the fly-past of 603 City of Edinburgh, 500 County of Kent, and 501 County of

Gloucester Squadrons of the R.A.A.F. That evening the Prince was guest of honour at the Welsh Guards Regimental Dinner at the Dorchester Hotel. Next morning he opened the Exhibition of Children's Playground Equipment and Layout organized by the London and Greater London Playing Fields Association at County Hall, Westminster.

Meanwhile the Queen gave audiences to more members of the Foreign Service, and in the afternoon, with Sir Leslie Boyce, Chairman of the King George VI Foundation, Mr W. McMillan, the sculptor, and Mr de Soissons, the architect, she inspected a model of the statue of her father and of the site it would occupy. On June 12 the Queen attended the Royal Naval Volunteer Reserve Jubilee Review on Horse Guards, and in the evening Prince Philip was guest of honour at the R.N.V.R. dinner at Royal Naval College, Greenwich. Both Her Majesty and Prince Philip welcomed the Pakistan and England cricket teams to Buckingham Palace at noon.

One of the most inspiring of modern Garter ceremonies took place on June 14, when Sir Winston Churchill was installed in St George's Chapel at Windsor. There was sunshine to mark the great day, so that the angled shadows of the ancient fortress, where so much of English history has been made and so much lies enshrined, were thrown across the foot-worn paths and the picturesque huddle of centuries-old houses beside the walls.

Lord Freyberg, V.C., led the Military Knights ot Windsor out of the Quadrangle as the procession set out; the tabarded Pursuivants, Heralds, and Provincial Kings of Arms came behind, and then the Noble Knights themselves in the rich majesty of their wonderful kingfisher-blue mantles and their great plumed hats. In twos they marched while the cheers of the onlookers came in waves of excitement as they recognized their favourites. In order of seniority reversed they came, and most junior of all and leading the way alone was Sir Winston—a knight in truth *sans peur et sans reproche*. Last of all came the Sovereign of the Order, Her Majesty, with Prince Philip as escort. They came to a thunderous roar of cheering all the way.

The long procession swung into Horseshoe Cloister and up the great staircase, where, at the head, it was met by the clergy of St George's, themselves members of the Order, with the Noble and Military Knights.

As the Sovereign of the Order passed into the chapel the trumpets rang out and sent their silver echoes about the stone vaulting and the cloistered beauty of the nave. Here on the stalls the armorial plates of the knights of England told a story of unbroken service for 600 years and more, and the richly coloured banners of the living knights hung still in the June air above the heads of those who now came to install yet another Noble Knight.

In wonderful white-and-gold dress stood the Queen—a slight figure, whose face now held dignity and authority and pride, but above all pride in the continuing strength of this tradition that was about to be proclaimed. Facing her in the choir stood Sir Winston Churchill and Lord Halifax, Chancellor of the Order. And watching it all, tense with excitement, was Prince Charles, dressed in a golden-yellow suit, who seemed to know that one day, when the title of Prince of Wales was his, he would be second only to the Sovereign in precedence in the Order.

The service began—a service in which for so short a time the Queen becomes Queen of England alone and all the majesty of her high position as head of the biggest Commonwealth of Nations the world has known is forgotten. Time is turned back and the oldest nation of the Commonwealth thanks God for the benisons of all the momentous years. And this day, in his own stall Sir Winston Churchill, already assured of his place in world history, came to his newest honour among the chivalry of England.

It was Royal Ascot again from June 15 until June 18, and the Queen was present on all four days. Again Aureole made the rainy days golden. He won the Hardwicke Stakes, and the Queen's colt, Landau, ridden by Sir Gordon Richards, won the Rous Memorial Stakes. But even Royal Ascot had to be interrupted on June 18 when Her Majesty received Herr Raab, the Austrian Chancellor.

While Prince Philip was in France and Germany the Queen was busy at the Palace. On June 22 she gave a luncheon to M. Vincent Auriol, the President of France, and Mme Auriol. Mme Auriol had come to England in connexion with the award to her husband of an Oxford degree, and Queen Elizabeth was glad to be able to renew the friendship and to discuss the latest developments of Anglo-French policy with her visitors. After lunch the Queen received Sir Gladwyn Jebb, new Ambassador to France, and later Mr Anthony Eden, the Foreign Secretary. That evening she had her weekly meeting with the Prime Minister at 6.30.

Prince Philip flew himself back to England in an R.A.F. Devon plane on June 27, and on the following day the King and Queen of Sweden arrived in London on a State visit. During the afternoon at the Palace the Queen conferred the Order of the Garter on King Gustaf VI Adolf. The following morning the Queen received at noon the Duke of Hamilton and Brandon, who reported, as Lord High Commissioner to the General Assembly of the

Church of Scotland, on the deliberations and work of the Assembly. At 11 A.M. the same day Prince Philip went to St Mary's Hospital, Paddington, to make a presentation to Sir Alexander Fleming to commemorate the twenty-fifth anniversary of the discovery of penicillin. After lunch the Queen sat for her portrait to Mr Simon Elwes, and at 6.30 she received the Chancellor of the Exchequer, Mr R. A. Butler. Later that evening, with the Prince, Her Majesty attended a private dinner at the Swedish Embassy with the King and Queen of Sweden. The Swedish State visit ended on July 1.

On July 6 the Queen inspected the Yeomen of the Guard in the garden at Buckingham Palace. Six officers, six sergeant-majors, and sixty-one yeomen of the Queen's Body Guard were present then with Lord Onslow, commander of the Yeomen, at forty-one the youngest on parade. As Captain, Lord Onslow was the only political appointment in the Guard, for all other officers are appointed by the Sovereign. For this reason the Guard's Lieutenant, or second officer, Major-General Sir Allan Adair, is its permanent commanding officer.

At 2.30 P.M. the same day Her Majesty received in audience Mrs Pandit, sister of Jawaharlal Nehru, the Indian Prime Minister. Mrs Pandit, the Indian delegate to the United Nations for some years and former Indian Ambassador to Moscow and Washington, was on her way to take over the presidency of the General Assembly of the United Nations, the first woman to hold this post. The Queen seized the opportunity of the visit to acquaint herself with the latest news from India.

The Royal Agricultural Show opened at Windsor on July 7, and on that day the Dartmoor Pony Society, through the three little daughters of Lieutenant-Colonel and Mrs J. F. S. Bullen, of Charmouth, Dorset, presented the Queen with a brown gelding pony of eleven hands named Juniper. This four-year-old pony was for Prince Charles. On the following day at the National Coal Board's stand Her Majesty recognized a fifteen-year-old bay gelding pit pony named Dunn which had been at Newton Royal Show two years before. It had then had one of its legs bandaged, having been kicked by a stray horse the night before. Now the Queen spoke with Mr J. S. Duckmanton, East Midlands Division horse inspector, recalling that she had seen it when injured and inquiring if it was fully recovered.

On July 9 Prince Philip joined *Britannia* for Cowes Regatta, and after racing *Bluebottle* there he set out for Dartmouth and a visit to the Royal Naval College, where, as a cadet, he had first met Princess Elizabeth during the War.

The police forces of the United Kingdom sent representatives to a great review in Hyde Park on July 14, when both the Queen and Prince Philip were present. That morning Her Majesty had received Mr Somerset Maugham, the distinguished novelist and playwright, at Buckingham Palace and invested him with the insignia of a Companion of Honour.

The Lieutenants of Counties—for the first time this century—entertained their Sovereign to dinner on July 15. The Queen, accompanied by Prince Philip, dined in the Great Gallery of Lancaster House with ninety of her Lieutenants. The tables were glittering with the silver and gold plate which had been lent by the hosts of the evening. Among it was plate presented to the first Duke of Marlborough, now lent by Earl Spencer, and said to be among the finest in the world. After dinner Her Majesty accepted as a gift a painting, by Terence Cuneo, of Prince Philip's act of homage during the Coronation ceremony.

With the victory of Aureole in the King George VI and Queen Elizabeth Stakes at the second Ascot meeting on July 17 the Queen became the leading owner in Britain for 1954. Aureole won the richest prize in British racing—£23,302—thus bringing Her Majesty's winnings for the season to £35,799. The Queen was delighted at Aureole's success, for she had always had faith in the horse while others had often decried it, and the crowd watching her as she made her way to the unsaddling enclosure after Aureole had held off a strong challenge from an international field saw how happy she was and gave her an ovation.

On July 19 Prince Philip held the first meeting in connexion with his great project on the Social Responsibility of Industry. To Buckingham Palace came industrialists and trade unionists to discuss plans for a conference on the social responsibility of industry throughout the Commonwealth and Empire to be organized by the Industrial Welfare Society, of which Prince Philip is patron.

The vital necessity to study the social problems of industry had been in Prince Philip's mind for some years, and in this he had the fullest support of the Queen. But there had been difficulties in organizing the meeting—suspicions in some minds as to the motives and a fear among some trade unionists that such a conference might be used by some industrialists as a means of gaining concessions from the workers. In view of all this Prince Philip had to proceed cautiously. The first meeting at Buckingham Palace, therefore, was private. Afterwards it was announced that a three-week conference would be held at Oxford in July 1956. "There is no suggestion that there should be consideration and discussion of the formal relationships between employers and trade unions, covering wages, conciliation, and arbitration machinery," the statement ended.

At 1 P.M. the same day the Queen with Prince Philip entertained Prince Bernhard of the Netherlands and his three daughters, Princess Beatrix, Princess Irene, and Princess Margriet, to luncheon at the Palace, the first time the Royal Family had met the little princesses. Prince Charles and Princess Anne were also there.

The following day Prince Philip dined with the High Commissioner for Canada, Mr Norman Robertson, and discussed with him the final details of the Canadian tour.

On July 21 His Royal Highness presided at the annual meeting of the Automobile Association. Prince Philip soon showed that he had no intention of being just a President in name. He took to ringing up the headquarters of the Association whenever he saw, on his travels, traffic-handling methods which he thought might be adopted with advantage in Britain. Hardly a week passed without the Prince ringing to suggest new spots where A.A. boxes might be sited on roads where they would be most useful for motorists. On his visits to the headquarters of the Association he also made suggestions for saving work and costs.

Her Majesty's Body Guard of the Honorable Corps of Gentlemen-at-Arms entertained the Queen and Prince Philip at a mess dinner at St James's Palace on July 22. This was the first time a reigning sovereign had been entertained to dinner by the Corps, despite the fact that it had been in existence for 445 years since its foundation by Henry VIII as "The Gentlemen Speres." The royal guests were met by the guard's four officers (the Captain, Colonel the Earl Fortescue; the Lieutenant, Brigadier-General Sir Harvey Kearsley; the Standard Bearer, Lieutenant-Colonel the Hon. O. E. Vesey; Clerk of the Cheque and Adjutant, Lieutenant-Colonel the Marquess of Ormonde) and by the Harbinger (Major-General A. R. Chater). The Gentlemen and their officers wore the traditional evening dress of the Household: dark-blue evening coats with black velvet collar and flat gilt buttons engraved with the royal cipher and Imperial Crown.

The Comte and Comtesse de Paris (the Comte is Pretender to the French Throne) came to Buckingham Palace to tea on August 3 on one of their rare appearances in London. Four days later Her Majesty flew to Balmoral for the usual summer stay. But on August 17 she travelled to Belfast to launch the new Shaw Savill and Albion liner, *Southern Cross*, a promise she had made after the same company's *Gothic* had been selected as the royal yacht for the Commonwealth tour in 1953–54.

September 9 saw the Queen at the Braemar Highland Games—much-changed Games since the days when Queen Victoria made them an important part of the summer royal engagements. In those days Queen Victoria used to watch the race up Craig Cheunnick, until she learned how gruelling it was, and so forbade it. On October 9 Her Majesty attended the Balaclava Centenary celebrations of the Argyll and Sutherland Highlanders at Stirling Castle. This was the first of a series of such celebrations. After the return of the Royal Family to London on October 10 there were other occasions.

On November 20 in Deene Park, the 400-year-old home of the seventh Earl of Cardigan, who led the Charge of the Light Brigade at Balaclava, Prince Philip and the Duke of Gloucester were guests at a historic dinner. Present were descendants of the Earl of Cardigan and of the other British commanders at the battle, Lords Raglan and Lucan, and of Lord Tennyson, whose poem immortalized the Charge. Around the room were souvenirs of the great battle, the head and tail of Ronald, the charger which carried the Earl of Cardigan into battle, and his uniform.

On November 26 the Queen, Prince Philip, and the Queen Mother attended the Balaclava Ball at the Hyde Park Hotel, London, given by the officers of the 4th, 8th, 11th, and 13th/18th Hussars and the 17th/21st Lancers, whose regiments made the Charge. Officers were permitted, in view of the historic occasion, to wear the full dress uniform of dark-blue tunics laced with silver or gold 'tights' and Russian boots decorated with rosettes.

Major-General J. F. B. Combe, Colonel of the 11th Hussars, wore the actual tunic and slung jacket worn by the Earl of Cardigan in the Charge and also carried his sword.

After the holiday in Scotland the Queen and Prince Philip were in London for the State visit of the Emperor of Ethiopia on October 14. Emperor Haile Selassie was no stranger to London, and the London crowds had not forgotten his stay in Britain during his exile before and during the War. At Buckingham Palace the Queen conferred on the Emperor the Order of the Garter and on his son, the Duke of Harar, the insignia of Knight Grand Cross of the Royal Victorian Order. Haile Selassie gave to Her Majesty the Chain of the Order of the Seal of Solomon and to Prince Philip the Chain of the Most Exalted Order of the Queen of Sheba.

The Queen had produced a sensation in many quarters on October 8, when the Duke of Norfolk, as Her Majesty's representative, made it known that in the new, larger, and renamed Royal Enclosure being built at Ascot the Court rules governing divorce would cease to be applied. But, the announcement continued, entry to the Queen's Lawn, which would be a small area within the Royal Enclosure, would be by invitation, and the Court rules governing divorce would apply.

On October 20 Her Majesty entertained to lunch at the Palace King Feisal of Iraq and the Crown Prince. The same day the Queen conferred on Mr Anthony Eden a Knighthood of the Order of the Garter.

With Prince Philip the Queen set out on October 21 on a two-day visit to Lancashire. Back in London the Queen received Mr Yoshida, Prime Minister of Japan, on October 26, and on the following day she set out with Prince Philip for a four-day visit to the West Riding of Yorkshire, Northumberland, and Durham. Back in London again on November 1 Her Majesty gave lunch at the Palace to Crown Prince Olaf of Norway, and in the evening, with Prince Philip and Princess Margaret, she attended the annual performance of the Variety Artistes Benevolent Fund.

Throughout November and December the Queen was busy every day receiving members of the Cabinet, of the military and foreign services, and overseas visitors. On November 9 Her Majesty received Sayed Ismail el Azhari, Prime Minister of the Sudan. On November 16 Mr M. A. H. Ispahani, retiring High Commissioner for Pakistan, came to the Palace to say his farewells. On December 16 Her Majesty received Mr C. D. Howe, Minister of Trade and Commerce for Canada, and on December 20 one visitor was the King of Jordan. On December 21 Mrs Pandit came again, this time on her appointment as India's High Commissioner to the United Kingdom. The same day M. Massigli, long-time French Ambassador to London, came to say farewell and was appointed Companion of Honour by the Queen.

The Queen received Professor Albert Richardson, the new President of the Royal Academy, and Mr H. Brooks, the Secretary, on December 16. The President was surprised to learn that Her Majesty knew the contents of the speech he had made at the Royal Academy the day before. The Queen asked him about his 'must' collection which he carries in his pocket—a paintbox smaller than a diary, a snuffbox, a compass, a folding doorkey, a penknife, and spare spectacles. Later the Queen went to the Academy to see the exhibition of eighteenth-century masters.

"The Queen walked round every gallery while the public were inside," said Professor Richardson. "I had intended to tell her about each picture. Instead she told me, and I did nearly all the listening.

"She is amazing. She talked about compositions and the derivation of exhibits. I could not add to her knowledge.

"We have to go back to George III to find a reigning King or Queen to equal her knowledge. At one point Her Majesty paused before an interior of Buckingham Palace and, pointing to a clock, said, 'That was there in Queen Charlotte's time. It is still there.' "

There had been the ceremonial State opening of Parliament on November 30. There were the services connected with Remembrance Day and the preparations for Christmas. In all these things the visits to Buckingham Palace of the Governors of the Northern and Eastern Provinces of Nigeria passed unnoticed. But at these meetings Her Majesty first discussed the possibilities of a tour of the largest of the African countries in point of population.

13

A Year of Visitors

It is at Sandringham at Christmas that the Queen finds it most easy to relax and to live a life more like that of an ordinary citizen. There she can mix with the villagers in her position as 'squire,' can visit the local organizations such as the Women's Institute, and can be almost free from public attention.

But 1955 was different from most years. The Queen held a Privy Council meeting at Sandringham on January 5; it was the first entry in the engagement diary for the year. Among those present were Lord Salisbury (Lord President), Mr Gwilym Lloyd-George (Home Secretary), and Mr R. A. Butler (Chancellor of the Exchequer), and the business discussed was the rail strike threatened for the following Sunday and the measures to be adopted if it materialized.

For the rest of the month the Queen carried out the usual duties of her annual stay at Sandringham. She received a visit from schoolboys (this time eleven pupils of Hammonds Grammar School, Swaffham, with their headmaster) on January 16, and presented Sunday-school prizes at West Newton School on January 22.

The holiday was interrupted on January 31. On that day the Queen returned to Buckingham Palace from Norfolk to lunch with her sister before Princess Margaret left for her West Indies tour. Afterwards Her Majesty returned to Sandringham.

February opened with a burst of political activity, for the Commonwealth Prime Ministers were in London again, and there was still the threat of a rail shut-down.

On February 1 Her Majesty held a Privy Council at Buckingham Palace, and the members present included Lord Salisbury, Mr Harry Crookshank (Lord Privy Seal), Lord Reading (Minister of State at the Foreign Office), Mr Osbert Peake (Minister of Pensions), and Mr Selwyn Lloyd (Minister of Supply). Among the business discussed was the nuclear-power programme of electrical generating stations.

At 10.45 A.M. Her Majesty presented the insignia of Companion of Honour to Mr Harry Crookshank. A Privy Council was held at 10.30 A.M. At 11.30 A.M. the Queen received Mr T. C. Webb, High Commissioner for New Zealand, and Mrs Webb. At twelve noon the Right Rev. Harry Carpenter paid homage on appointment as Bishop of Oxford. At 12.30 P.M. Mr Mohammed Ikramullah came to the Palace on his appointment as High Commissioner for Pakistan in London. At 5.30 P.M. there was the usual weekly audience for the Prime Minister.

The Queen sat to Annigoni in the Yellow Drawing Room at the Palace at 11 A.M. on February 2. At 2.30 P.M. Her Majesty received Mr R. G. Menzies, Prime Minister of Australia, and at 3.15 P.M. Sir John Kotelawala, Prime Minister of Ceylon, came to the Palace for an audience. At 6 P.M. Mr Louis St Laurent, Prime Minister of Canada, was received in audience. Later Her Majesty, with Prince Philip, gave a dinner for all the Prime Ministers attending the Commonwealth Conference.

The engagements for February 3 opened with an audience

for the Lord Chamberlain. At noon the Queen saw the new Italian Ambassador, Count Vittorio Zoppi. At 12.15 P.M. Mr S. G. Holland, Prime Minister of New Zealand, came to see the Queen. At 2.30 P.M. Pandit Nehru, Prime Minister of India, was received in audience. At 5.55 P.M. Her Majesty presented Miss Dorothy Meynell with the medal of Member of the Royal Victorian Order (Fourth Class), and at 6 P.M. the Queen and Prince Philip gave a party for the staffs of the delegations at the Conference.

On February 4 at 2.30 P.M. the Queen saw Mr C. R. Swart, Minister of Justice for South Africa, who had represented his country at the Conference, and at 3.15 P.M. Mr Mohammed Ali, the Pakistan Prime Minister, had an audience of Her Majesty.

On February 16 Signor Scelba, the Italian Prime Minister, with Signora Scelba and Signor Martino, Italian Foreign Minister, was received by the Queen at Buckingham Palace, and Her Majesty, apart from commenting on the business of the visitors in London—they had come for talks with the British Government on European unity—ranged over a wide variety of subjects in her conversation. In questioning Signora Scelba about her welfare work in Italy the Queen gave her own views on the care of children, and explained how she intended her own to be educated, revealing that Prince Charles would go to a boarding-school as soon as he was nine.

The Shah of Persia and Queen Soraya lunched with the Queen at the Palace on February 18, and on February 22 Her Majesty went to an evening party at the American Embassy as the guest of Mr Winthrop Aldrich, the Ambassador. This was the first big ambassadorial occasion in Winfield House since it had been given to the American nation as a home for its London embassy by Miss Barbara

Hutton, the Woolworth heiress. Winfield House, with its twelve acres of gardens, is, next to Buckingham Palace, the biggest private estate in London.

Princess Margaret returned to England on March 3 after a trip through the West Indies which was a complete triumph. The Queen, accompanied by Prince Philip, met her at London Airport.

When the Queen dined with Sir Winston and Lady Churchill at 10 Downing Street on April 4 the impending resignation of the great Prime Minister was already known to Her Majesty. Indeed, the engagement had been booked since early in the year, and the Queen had left the whole day free from official business. Prince Philip himself had only two engagements that day—a short sitting to Mr Edward Halliday in the Centre Room at Buckingham Palace at 4 P.M. and a meeting at 4.30 P.M. in connexion with his "Duke of Edinburgh's Badge Award" to youth.

Never before had a Queen dined with her Prime Minister at his official residence.

"Having served in office or in Parliament under four sovereigns who have reigned since those days [when Sir Winston was a cavalry subaltern in the reign of Queen Victoria], I felt, with these credentials, that in asking Your Majesty's gracious permission to propose this toast I should not be leading to the creation of a precedent which would often cause inconvenience," said Sir Winston, in proposing the Queen's health. "Madam, I should like to express the deep and lively sense of gratitude which we and all your peoples feel to you and His Royal Highness, the Duke of Edinburgh, for all the help and inspiration we receive in our daily lives, and which spreads with ever-growing strength throughout the British realm and the Commonwealth and Empire.

"Never have the august duties which fall upon the British monarchy been discharged with more devotion than in the brilliant opening of Your Majesty's reign. We thank God for the gift he has bestowed upon us, and vow ourselves anew to the sacred causes and wise and kindly way of life of which Your Majesty is the young, gleaming champion."

In return Her Majesty proposed the health of Sir Winston.

It was on the following day that the resignation was announced. Sir Winston Churchill drove to Buckingham Palace to see the Queen at 4.30 P.M., and in half an hour the great statesman had handed over his office and said his official farewells.

The fact that none of London's national newspapers was being published on account of the strike of printing staffs reduced the public notice of the passing from office of Sir Winston, but it did not minimize the interest of the outside world. While there was really no doubt who would succeed Sir Winston, it was not until April 6 that the Queen sent for Sir Anthony Eden—at 11 A.M.—and offered him the post of Prime Minister.

On April 7 the Queen held a Privy Council at Buckingham Palace at which Mr Lennox-Boyd (Colonial Secretary), Mr Heathcoat-Amory (Minister of Agriculture and Food), and Mr J. Boyd-Carpenter (Minister of Transport) were present. Later Her Majesty distributed the Royal Maundy. This year the ceremony took place at Southwark Cathedral. In 1953, because of structural alterations at Westminster Abbey, the Queen had distributed the Maundy Money at St Paul's Cathedral. The innovation was so successful that Her Majesty decided that in future other cathedrals should stage the ceremony, thus reverting to a custom which had lapsed in the time of Charles II. In the evening, with Prince Philip, the Queen Mother, and Princess Margaret, Queen Elizabeth went into residence at Windsor Castle. There, on April 12, she received the Prime Minister at 3 P.M. and held another Council half an hour later. The following day, accompanied by Prince Philip, Her Majesty set off to tour North Lancashire.

There was an engagement at Ascot Racecourse on April 20, when the Queen drove over from Windsor to inspect the alterations, which included an entirely new course, a doubled paddock, and enclosures, including the Royal Enclosure (with the Queen's Lawn), two new luncheon rooms, a children's playground with staff, and many more seats for tired racegoers. In fact Royal Ascot had to be postponed owing to the rail strike, but the Queen, as the owner, was anxious to be sure that all the improvements would be finished in time for the opening.

On April 23 Queen Elizabeth drove to the National Stud at Gillingham, Dorset, to inspect some of the colts and fillies which would be available for racing as two-year-olds in 1956. Two colts and six fillies were with their mothers in the paddocks. Her Majesty saw the filly by Krakatao out of Sun Chariot which later received the name of Woomera; the colt by Tudor Minstrel out of Enchanted Forest whose name was to become Great Birnam; the unfortunate Troika, which had to be destroyed after an accident in 1956; the filly by Big Game out of Mombasa named Impala; another which received the name of Anthracite and was by Abernant out of Fair Profit; one by Tenerani out of Cretan Belle which received the name of Ten Bells; and the filly by Blue Peter out of Game Court to be named Deck Tennis. But the filly which caught Her Majesty's eye most was one by Dante out of Calash. The Queen provisionally booked all eight yearlings, but most especially the Dante-Calash filly, which she afterwards named Carozza. It was with this filly that Her Majesty won the 1957 Oaks—complete justification for her choice on that April day in 1955.

At the same time that she selected Carozza as a likely classic winner the Queen was beginning to show interest in a filly she had bred herself at the royal stud at Hampton Court. Mulberry Harbour had looked as promising as Carozza, but in the 1957 Oaks, though she was the choice of the Queen's first jockey, Harry Carr, it was the second choice, Carozza, with Lester Piggott up, which came through to win.

Five days after her visit to the National Stud the Queen gave further evidence of her great interest in horses and horse-breeding by visiting the Equine Research Establishment at Ballaton Lodge, Newmarket. This establishment is run by the Animal Health Trust, whose founder and scientific director is Dr W. R. Wooldridge. Dr Wooldridge has often expressed the view that undue 'coddling' is bad for animals. This is a view shared by the Queen.

At Hampton Court (known as the Sandringham stud, where the stud once was located) the brood mares and stallions and the foals are allowed out into the open as much as possible. The stallions and mares run in the paddocks in rough coats, and, when the weather is kind, are often allowed to remain outdoors all night. Yet when hot sunshine brings myriads of flies to the paddock the mares and foals are often kept indoors until the evening. The grooms are encouraged to make friends with the foals at the earliest opportunity—the second or third day after their birth—and a few days later the youngsters are introduced to a head-collar. Her Majesty believes that this has a great effect on the psychological make-up of the horses later on.

The Portuguese Ambassador, Senhor Pedro Pereira, drove to the Palace at 11.45 A.M. on May 12 to present a letter to the Queen from the President of Portugal in connexion with the projected visit to London in the following October of the President and Senhora Lopes.

The European Horse Trials opened in Windsor Great Park, at the Queen's invitation, on May 18, and Her Majesty, a visitor on all three days, saw Major (now Lieutenant-Colonel) Frank Weldon on Kilberry become the individual winner, with Lieutenant-Commander J. Oram on Radar second and Mr A. E. Hill on Countryman (which later the Queen bought) third.

When the Aga Khan went to Buckingham Palace at 12.50 on May 26 to receive the insignia of Knight Grand Cross of the Order of St Michael and St George it was recalled that he had received his first knighthood—Knight Commander of the Indian Empire—from Queen Victoria in 1898. "Her Majesty observed that, since I was a prince myself and the descendant of kings, she would not ask me to kneel to receive the accolade and the touch of the sword on my shoulder, but she would simply hand the order to me," the Aga Khan said. "I was greatly touched by her consideration and courtesy." At the ceremony on May 26 Queen Elizabeth followed the example of her great-great-grandmother.

At 4.30 P.M. on the same day the Queen drove to the studio of Mr Terence Cuneo to view, with Mr Michael Hornby, Prime Warden of the Goldsmiths Company, the portrait of Her Majesty commissioned by the Company.

The Queen was at Balmoral between May 28 and June 5. While she was there she presented new colours to the

1st Battalion Queen's Own Cameron Highlanders on May 30, and held a Privy Council meeting on May 31 at which the Councillors were the Marquess of Salisbury, the Earl of Munster (Minister without Portfolio), and Mr Geoffrey Lloyd (Minister of Fuel and Power). Her Majesty signed the proclamation of a State of Emergency to cope with the problem of maintaining essential services during the rail strike.

Back in London again the Queen visited the Antique Dealers' Fair on June 7. As usual, the Royal Family had sent exhibits. Her Majesty's contribution this year was the Table of Commanders of Sèvres porcelain with ormolu mounts made for Napoleon I in 1812 and presented by Louis XVIII to the Prince Regent in 1817. On June 8, with Prince Philip, Her Majesty attended the Royal Tournament at Olympia, and Nuri es Said Pasha, Prime Minister of Iraq, who had been received by the Queen earlier, was also present in the royal box.

There was a very subdued opening of Parliament on June 9, for, owing to the rail strike, the carriage procession was dispensed with. The annual Trooping the Colour ceremony on June 9 was also cancelled.

The Queen knighted and invested with the insignia of Knight Commander of the Royal Victorian Order Major Crocker Bulteel, Clerk of the Course at Ascot, and Mr Eric Savill, Deputy Ranger of Windsor Park, on June 17, and afterwards gave them lunch at Windsor Castle. On the same morning Her Majesty conferred M.V.O.'s and Royal Victorian Medals on a number of the royal staff. On June 18 the King and Queen of Jordan came to the Castle for dinner and remained overnight.

Prior to her State visit to Norway—her first foreign visit since her accession—the Queen named the new

Canadian Pacific liner, *Empress of Britain*, at its launching on June 22 from the Fairfield Yard on the Clyde. This was the second merchant ship Her Majesty had named, and she is the only reigning British sovereign to have carried out such a task. Later that day, after the naming ceremony, the Queen, with Prince Philip, boarded the royal yacht *Britannia* at Rosyth for the trip across the North Sea to Norway.

On their return from Norway on June 29 the Queen, with Prince Philip, carried out engagements in Dundee and Edinburgh and went into residence in the Palace of Holyroodhouse. On their way back to London they stopped at Nottingham for a visit to the Royal Show on July 6. On July 19 Her Majesty paid her first visit to Kennington Oval, part of the Duchy of Cornwall lands, when she saw Surrey playing against the South Africans. The Queen went to Winchester on July 25 to celebrate the two hundredth anniversary of the foundation of the King's Royal Rifle Corps (60th Rifles) in America. There she spoke to four of the seventeen Americans who had fought with the regiment as volunteers until America entered the War in 1941.

After the Queen with Prince Philip had toured Wales, the Isle of Man, and Wigtownshire, between August 6 and 10, the royal yacht *Britannia* carried them round the north of Scotland to Aberdeen on August 13. On that day the Balmoral holiday began, and, apart from an unusual sale of work on August 20 at Abergeldy Castle in aid of Crathie Church, at which the Queen, Prince Philip, Prince Charles, and Princess Anne assisted the Queen Mother, who had organized it, there were almost no public engagements.

The Queen went to Doncaster on September 7 for the St Leger, and on the following day, after a Council at

The Queen went to London Airport in July 1957 to say farewell to her mother when Queen Elizabeth left for a tour of Central Africa.

The most glittering banquet ever held in the city was how New York welcomed Queen Elizabeth II and Prince Philip in October 1957. Here, at the dinner given by the Pilgrims and the English-Speaking Union, Mr Lewis Douglas, former American Ambassador to the Court of St James's, shares a joke with the Queen.

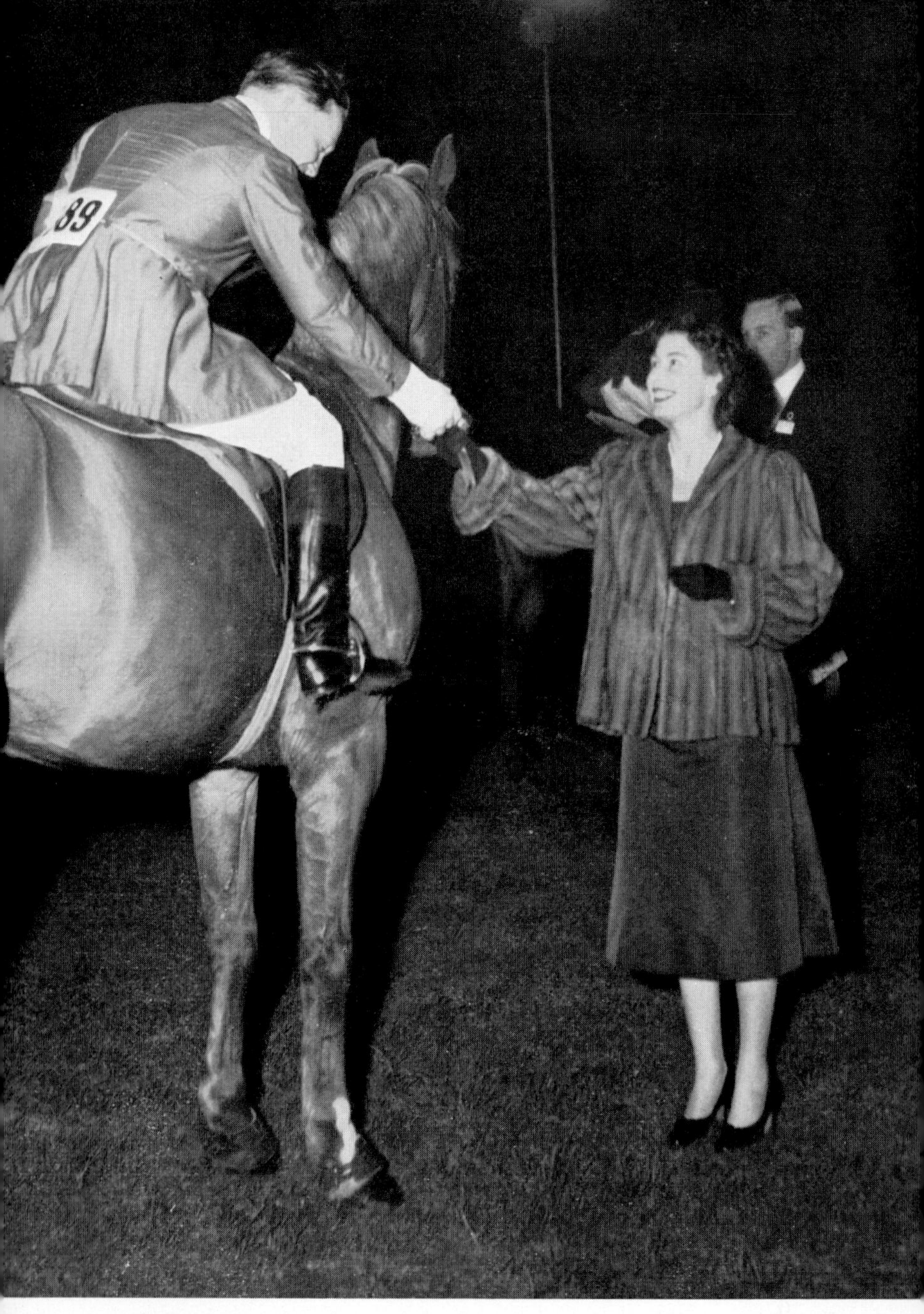

Royal Windsor Horse Show is one of the favourite engagements of Her Majesty the Queen. Here Queen Elizabeth is seen presenting a second-prize rosette to Mr Derek Kent, riding Gay Romance at the May 1956 Show.

Balmoral, she drove with her family to the Braemar Games. On October 1 the Prime Minister and Lady Eden travelled to Balmoral to stay with the Queen. Her Majesty was back in London on October 17.

It was while the Royal Family was at Balmoral that the *Monthly Record*, magazine of the Free Church of Scotland, came out with strong criticism of Prince Philip for playing polo on Sunday, cricket on two Sundays in July, and of the Queen and other members of the Royal Family for watching. "We cannot imagine Her Gracious Majesty the Queen willingly stepping aside to give this needless hurt to the conscience of many thousands . . . it is surely quite clear to those in authority in Church and State, who have the ear of the Royal Household, that a blow struck at the sacred convictions of millions in the Commonwealth is undoubtedly a blow at the foundations of the Throne and a strengthening of the anarchy that would sweep away all rule and order in our land."

The attack was met with immediate rebuffs from all parts of the country and the world, but it once again revealed the constant limelighting of all royal actions, and yet showed that in so rarely being the object of criticism the Queen and the Royal Family were setting an amazing example of selfless service.

On October 19 the Queen, accompanied by Prince Philip, the Queen Mother, and Princess Margaret, attended the service at Lambeth Palace for the rededication of the 700-year-old chapel, which had been almost entirely destroyed by aerial attack during the War.

The national memorial statue of King George VI in Carlton Gardens was unveiled by Her Majesty on October 21, a day of driving rain and chill winds. Queen Elizabeth spoke of her father in warming tones. "His fortitude, determination, and confidence throughout the perilous summer of 1940 and the anxious years that followed were an inspiration to all who loved freedom. He was the living symbol of our steadfastness. . . . The friendliness and simplicity which so endeared him to his peoples during the trials of war were the fruit of a lifelong interest in his fellow-men and of a human sympathy which was one of my father's most lovable qualities," said the Queen.

"Much was asked of my father in personal sacrifice and endeavour, often in the face of illness; his courage in overcoming it endeared him to everybody. He shirked no task, however difficult, and to the end he never faltered in his duty to his peoples."

That evening in the Painted Hall of the Royal Naval College at Greenwich the Queen, by attending the Trafalgar Day dinner with the Lords Commissioners of the Admiralty, became the first reigning Queen ever to dine at the College.

General Craveiro Lopes, President of Portugal, and Senhora Lopes came to London on October 25, to a reception from large crowds which must have convinced them that the 800-year-old links between Portugal and Britain were still strong. At night at a banquet in the State Ballroom at Buckingham Palace the Queen entertained the visitors. On either side of the room throughout its length was a wonderful display of the gold vases, platters, and flagons in the Palace collection, including the gold vase which was the Portuguese President's Coronation gift to the Queen. "The ancient alliance between us is founded on the Treaty which was signed in London in 1373 and was confirmed in the Treaty of Windsor in 1386. But our friendship is at least two hundred years older than our formal alliance," said the Queen.

General Lopes and Mme Lopes became close friends of Prince Charles and Princess Anne, and the visitors from Portugal were so attracted by the little Princess that they seized every opportunity to find time to play with her. One of the results of these many meetings was that after their return to Portugal they sent a two-foot-high doll with eight complete outfits of clothes, representing the local costumes of eight Portuguese provinces, for Princess Anne.

As the year came to a close Her Majesty was making her preparations for the visit with Prince Philip to Nigeria in January 1956. Her Nigerian Equerry, Major J. Aguiyi-Ironsi, of the Nigeria Regiment, had been appointed on December 6, when the Queen received him at the Palace. Throughout the month he was busy learning his duties, and accompanied Her Majesty when she went to the British Council's residence for colonial students in Hans Crescent.

At the year's end the Queen could look back on twelve months of continual State business and diplomatic activity. During the year Her Majesty received in audience the Prime Ministers of Australia, Canada, New Zealand, Ceylon, India, Malta, Pakistan, and Rhodesia, the Governors or Governors-General of Gibraltar, Trinidad, Windward Islands, British Columbia, Nigeria, Singapore, Pakistan, Canada, British Honduras, Cyprus, and Nyasaland. There was a constant stream of British Ambassadors and Ministers coming to the Palace to kiss hands on appointment and of foreign Ambassadors to the Court of St James's presenting their letters of credence to the Queen. Her Majesty saw her representatives in Lisbon, Panama, Monrovia, Oslo, Katmandu, Riyadh, The Hague, Quito, Manila, Ciudad Trujillo, Prague, Pnom Penh, Sofia, Washington, Dublin,

Damascus, Tegucigalpa, Brussels, Caracas, Budapest, Beirut, Luxembourg, Montevideo, Stockholm, Bangkok, and Bogota; the Australian Envoys to France and Egypt. From overseas came the representatives of Italy, Paraguay, Switzerland, Ecuador, France, Austria, Finland, Libya, Mexico, Nepal, Cambodia, Portugal, Czechoslovakia, Burma, Costa Rica, Japan, Egypt, Turkey, Luxembourg, Lebanon, the Argentine, and Laos. And there were a great many visits from members of the Foreign Service on retirement.

All these helped to make up the total of 467 official engagements which the Queen carried out during the year.

14

The Tropics and the North

QUEEN ELIZABETH, accompanied by Prince Philip, left London Airport at 4 P.M. on January 27, 1956, for the visit to Nigeria. Ahead lay one of the most important journeys of the Queen's life, for Nigeria, largest of Britain's colonies and the largest African territory in point of population, was in the throes of a campaign for independence within the Commonwealth, yet was divided by regional loyalties which made the attainment of Federal unity difficult. Her Majesty's visit was intended to demonstrate that people of differing creeds and customs could work together in harmony in a framework of Governments which had the Queen as its head.

In the early days of January, before her departure, the Queen carried out the usual activities of her holiday at Sandringham. But on January 10 she came back to London by train, arriving at Liverpool Street Station at 1.18 P.M. That evening the Prime Minister came to the Palace at 6.30 for his regular audience. The next day the Queen received Senhor Juscelino Kubitschek, President-elect of Brazil, and returned to Sandringham the following noon. She was back in London again on January 23, and on that day received Sir Anthony Eden at the Palace.

On January 24 there came to the Palace two other leaders of a British colony on the verge of independence—Tengku

(Prince) Abdul Rahman, the Chief Minister of Malaya, and Dato Bukit Gantang, Mentri Besar (Prime Minister) of the State of Perak. For half an hour the Queen talked of Malayan development and of the Commonwealth link.

A large number of Nigerians in their national dress were among the great crowd which gave the Queen and Prince Philip a memorable send-off from London Airport. Indeed, the demonstration was such as to merit a special "Thank you" from Her Majesty by radio from her plane as it crossed Europe.

The welcome by the people of Lagos to the royal travellers was fantastic in its enthusiasm. The Oba Adeniji-Adele II, hereditary ruler of Lagos, had ordered his chief medicine-man to "make powerful ju-ju" to ensure that the weather should be fine and clear for the Queen's arrival. And fine and clear it was. Later, on January 30, when a garden party was held at Government House, the sixty-two-year-old ruler claimed that he had ordered a short shower in order to clear the city of the humid heat which he thought might tax the Queen's strength despite the special cooling system which had been fitted to her room at Government House to ensure that at least she might sleep in a cool atmosphere. It rained for thirty-five minutes at the garden party, and rain was still falling when the Queen arrived. But the sun came out again before she left.

Among the first ceremonies in the Federal capital was the royal opening of the colony's Court of Appeal building. "The rule of law is vital to the freedom and orderly progress of any society, and we take special pride in the fact that in our Commonwealth the rule of law is maintained and that all men are equal in the eyes of the law.

For no society can be stable which is not based on this concept," the Queen told her audience.

It was a reminder to all Nigerians not only of the benefits of Commonwealth membership, but also of its obligations.

When the Queen and Prince Philip dined in state with twenty-two Nigerian Ministers and nobles at the end of the first day in the colony the royal party sat under a vast cream punka, the only one remaining in the country. There was something symbolic about this dinner—it demonstrated again the universal cover of the Queen's sovereignty.

Every hour of every day of the visit there were colour and excitement and triumph for the Queen. At Kaduna on February 2 Her Majesty made Malama Kuburu, thirty-three-year-old wife of a village blacksmith, a Member of the Order of the British Empire. The award was made for "Devoted Service to Women's Education in the Northern Region," but that citation covered a great fight to break down prejudices. Malama Kuburu was not only the first Moslem woman in Nigeria to be decorated by the Queen; she was also the only one who had 'stuck the course' in education.

When her name was called at the investiture Malama Kuburu stooped down quickly and removed her leather slippers before she walked towards the Queen. "I could not go to see Her Majesty with my shoes on—she is too great," she told those near her. "My heart was full of joy to be able to touch the Queen's hand and receive my medal," she said afterwards.

Her Majesty learned that Kuburu had had to fight the opposition of all the men in her village before she could follow her teaching career. She had her first child—a girl who is now studying at the Teachers' Training College at Sokoto—while still at college, but refused to give up her training.

"I took up teaching to help my country," she told the Queen.

It was at Kaduna that Her Majesty and Prince Philip held the tremendous durbar at which 8000 warriors in colourful dress came to show their loyalty. The fierce horsemen of the Jahi tribe charged at breakneck speed across the arena, pulling up only a few yards short of the covered daïs on which the Queen sat. Her Majesty told them, "This great concourse of men and horses has brought home to me the respect you have for your ancient traditions. I too respect those traditions, and hope that in a rapidly changing world you will maintain all that is good in them."

Below her were rainbow-hued garments of ancient times when the warrior hordes swept down out of the arid Sahara into the lush areas of Nigeria. Here were slender, eight-foot-long silver trumpets which were first blown centuries ago and cymbals whose brass was beaten before the first Elizabeth came to the throne of England.

At the Northern Region Parliament building on February 3 the Sardauna of Sokoto, Premier of the Region, spoke for chiefs and emirs of 18,000,000 Africans. "We are filled with joy and gladness at seeing so distinguished a successor to a line of kings and queens who have contributed so much to the unity of the free world during these times of stress and violence," he said.

The Queen asked those present to remember that, whatever difference there might be in religious beliefs, those beliefs form the background to the national standards of integrity and morality. "I am sure the Government of the Northern Region will always allow men freedom to worship God in the way the conscience of each dictates.

"Tolerance is necessary not only in religious matters, but also towards those whose views and traditions differ. It is by this spirit of understanding that the people of various races and tribes will be brought together," the Queen said.

At night on the floodlit lawns of the Governor's residence 200 dancers from four different provinces danced tribal dances to the beat of drums and the wail of pipes. Men from Benue Province, on twelve-foot-high stilts, advanced across the lawns in a fantastic Charleston, which showed an ancient method of escape from an enemy without leaving telltale footprints. Maingo tribesmen from the Jos Plateau, clad only in loincloths, red skull-caps, and coloured beads, danced with war axes in a tight circle. Bandawa dancers from Adamawa Province in black goatskins, beads, and iron anklets danced a Dodo, or evil-spirit dance. Here was evidence, if Her Majesty still needed it, of the complexity of the problem of unifying all Nigeria.

But the charm of the Queen and Prince Philip overcame every difficulty of tribe and creed and even of nationalism. Indeed, one of the greatest champions of Nigerian nationalism, Dr Nnamdi Azikiwe, Premier of the Eastern Region and leader of the most powerful political group in Nigeria, the National Council for Nigeria and the Cameroons, said at Enugu that he was disappointed by the welcome given to the Queen. "The crowds have been discouraged from giving a spontaneous reception by police and officials who have told them, 'Don't do this, don't do that,' instead of letting them give vent to their natural joy and excitement at seeing Her Majesty," he said.

The appearance of the Queen, in turquoise evening gown with magnificent diamond tiara, on the balcony of Enugu's House of Assembly, however, was sufficient to make a great crowd of Nigerians forget any inhibitions they may have had. At the Queen's appearance the roar of cheering was deafening.

At Calabar on February 8 women of the Efik tribe in multi-coloured hooped skirts, beaded yokes, and leggings studded with bells performed a rare ceremonial dance for the Queen. Each dancer held a red feather between her lips to signify silence and the solemnity of the occasion. In their hands they carried a *ntimi* (painted gourd) conveying messages of loyalty. Originally the *ntimi* dance was a symbol of such regal importance that the death penalty awaited anyone who should drop the gourd or misdirect its messages.

And so the royal progress continued. At Port Harcourt on the Bonny river, giant ninety-man war canoes raced past Her Majesty, and their brass cannon belched flame and thunderous sound. Musicians playing xylophones, bells, and drums and singers followed the war canoes in gaily decorated ceremonial gigs. In this hottest and most humid of Nigeria's towns the Queen appeared cool. One local resident said admiringly, "The Queen makes it seem like Westminster Pier in July. Yet this is the place where clothes go mouldy overnight, because they are always damp—and we've all got webbed feet."

A blind leper, Mr John Aguh, welcomed the royal party to the Oji River Settlement. "We wish to express our joy and happiness to Your Majesty and the Duke of Edinburgh for visiting this country and more especially this settlement. We are enjoying the shade and protection here of medicine and food. . . . Long live the Queen."

This was the first leper settlement ever visited by members of the Royal Family. Here the Queen met the ten-year-old girl and Prince Philip the thirteen-year-old boy whom they have adopted.

The supervisor of the settlement, Mr A. F. C. Savory, said, "The Queen's visit will do more to conquer man's fear and hate of the disease than any other single act I can think of. People all over the world will read that the Queen and the Duke penetrated a leper settlement, and this will convince them as nothing else could that most of their fears of the disease are groundless."

At Ibadan, capital of the Western Region and largest all-African city in the continent, to which the Queen travelled by train, Chief Obafemi Awolowo, Regional Premier, proclaimed the faith of the 7,000,000 people of the Region. "Nigeria is a British creation, and her security depends largely on the solidarity of the British Commonwealth," said Chief Awolowo. "Recognizing that the only symbol of this is the Queen, Nigerians pledge themselves to do all in their power to preserve the dignity, power, and privileges of the British Throne."

The Chief also declared the people's gratitude for the Queen's "devotion to all her subjects, whatever their creed, colour, clime, or race."

Though it was impossible to provide sizable guards for the royal travellers on their long journey, the visit to Nigeria passed almost without untoward incident. At Ibadan a Nigerian ex-soldier, Michael Tayo, with a supposed grievance against the local hospital authorities, tossed a letter of petition to the Queen through the open window of her car. Also at Ibadan, university students threatened a boycott of the visit because they had not been consulted about the arrangements. Prince Philip brought that 'mutiny' to an end by inquiring of a girl student, Florence Nwapa, "Are these boys behaving themselves?" The male students crowding round roared with laughter and joined in the welcome.

When she said good-bye to the people of Nigeria in a farewell broadcast from Lagos on February 15 Her Majesty referred to the signs of development on all sides. "But material progress by itself is not enough," said the Queen. "It is just as important that the conduct of our everyday life—in business, in industry, in the public service, and in Government—should come even closer to the ideals of honesty, integrity, and justice. Unless we maintain such standards the benefits of science and technology cannot be enjoyed."

Ten thousand masked and painted dancers, many of them on twelve-foot stilts, were among the million people who bade farewell at Lagos to the royal visitors. A rare performance of the fifteenth-century cult dance, the Adamu-Orisha play, figured among the demonstration. But it was the roar of cheers for "Our Queen" which showed more than anything how Her Majesty had won the hearts of the people. Observers decided that of all the enthusiastic receptions for the Queen they had experienced that from Nigerians generally was most overwhelming. In less than three weeks the Queen had turned a country which it had been expected would be lukewarm towards the visit into one in which every one was anxious to show his loyalty. In addition the visit had at last demonstrated to all Nigerians the possibility—until then still remote—that the three regions could be welded into a single country.

It was at Kano, on the edge of the Sahara, that the Queen and Prince Philip finally said farewell to Nigeria. Turbaned Moslem horsemen wearing armour which was made at the time of the Crusades formed a guard of honour for the royal visitors when they made a short tour of the mud-walled city which was once the greatest slave-trading port in all Africa. They were greeted by the Emirs of Kano, Gumel, Hadeija, and Kazure, and when finally the royal plane was ready to take off for London the Sardauna of Sokoto was there at the airport to say good-bye.

The Queen and Prince Philip arrived back in London on February 17. On February 21 Her Majesty held an investiture at Buckingham Palace and received the Prime Minister at 6.30 P.M. On the following day, with Prince Philip, the Queen Mother, and Princess Margaret, Her Majesty attended the "Welcome Home" luncheon of the City of London at Guildhall. February 23 saw official engagements back to normal pressure. At 11.40 A.M. the Queen received Lieutenant-General C. R. Hardy on his appointment as Commandant-General Royal Marines. At noon she received Air Marshal Sir Harry Broadhurst on his relinquishing the post of C.-in-C. Second Tactical Air Force. At 12.20 P.M. the Vice-Chamberlain presented an address from the House of Commons, and at 12.25 the Lord Chamberlain presented an address from the Lords. Her Majesty held a Council at 12.30, and at 12.45 she presented Wing Commander B. Horsley with the M.V.O. Fourth Class. At four o'clock the Queen visited the "English Taste in the Eighteenth Century" Exhibition at Burlington House. At 6.30 she received the Secretary of State for the Colonies to give him news of the great trip through Nigeria.

Prince Philip was with the Mediterranean Fleet from March 1 until March 10, and the Queen flew to Corsica to meet him on March 10. Thereafter the royal couple cruised in *Britannia* in Corsican waters for a week. They returned to London on March 18. For the rest of March and throughout April the Queen and her husband had a crowded list of engagements, which included laying the foundation stone of the new Coventry Cathedral and opening Chew Stoke Reservoir at Bristol.

Between April 18 and 20 the Queen was at Badminton for the Horse Trials, but she returned to Windsor Castle on the last day, and on April 22 entertained Mr Bulganin and Mr Khruschev, the Russian leaders, to tea in the Castle. On April 24 at Buckingham Palace Her Majesty invested Earl Attlee as a Knight of the Garter. On May 8 the Queen, with Prince Philip, visited Barnstaple, Exeter, and Torquay, and on the following day inspected Duchy of Cornwall property in Cornwall.

On May 11 the Queen, with Prince Philip, inaugurated a new-style private luncheon at the Palace designed to bring her into touch with every aspect of British life by giving her contact with leaders in every activity. The first guest list was made up of Major-General D. C. Spry, the Director-General of the Boy Scouts' International Bureau; Sir William Haley, Editor of *The Times*; the Right Rev. J. Montgomery Campbell, Bishop of London; Lord Aldenham, a banker; Sir Frank Lee, a civil servant, and two members of the Royal Household. Her Majesty held a second luncheon party on May 15, at which the guest list included Lord David Cecil; Sir Oliver Franks, a banker; Sir Arthur Elvin, Managing Director of Wembley Stadium; Mr Robert Birley, Headmaster of Eton; Mr James Bowman, chairman of the National Coal Board and once a miner at the coal-face; the Rev. S. Austin Williams, Vicar of St Martin's-in-the-Fields; and Sir Arthur Bliss, Master of the Queen's Musick. Her Majesty has been holding these luncheons at intervals ever since, and has found that through informal conversation at the table she can gather the most valuable background for her everyday work.

In the afternoon ex-King Leopold of the Belgians came to Buckingham Palace to take tea with the Queen. This was Leopold's first personal contact with the Royal Family since the early days of the last war. The visit was a sign that the estrangement between the two royal families which had existed since the Belgian capitulation in 1940 could now be considered at an end.

After her short visit to Balmoral between May 18 and May 27 the Queen returned to London to take the salute at the Trooping the Colour ceremony at 11 A.M. on May 31. Two hours later she took the salute at the R.A.F. fly-past from the balcony at Buckingham Palace.

When her Majesty had boarded the train at Aberdeen the most stringent security precautions were taken. No visitors were allowed on the platform, no photographers, no reporters. It was said that news had been received by the police that Cypriot terrorists were in the neighbourhood. But the Queen, to the delight of the large crowd waiting to say farewell, appeared suddenly on the observation platform of the last coach and was given a tremendous cheer.

In the evening of June 1 the Queen, with Prince Philip and Princess Margaret, attended a reception and ball given by the Grenadier Guards at 23 Knightsbridge.

On May 28 the Queen, accompanied by Prince Philip, the Queen Mother, Princess Margaret, the Duke of Gloucester, the Princess Royal, and other members of the Royal Family, had opened the Household Brigade Memorial Cloisters in Birdcage Walk, and in the evening the Queen was at the 1st Guards Club Dinner at the

Dorchester Hotel. That same day at noon Her Majesty had received in audience Dr Radhakrishnan, Vice-President of India. On June 4, after a visit to Stockton-on-Tees and Middlesbrough, the Queen and Prince Philip sailed in the royal yacht *Britannia* for the State visit to Sweden from June 8 until June 17.

The visit to Sweden demonstrated, apart from the very great affection expressed by the Swedes for the royal visitors, the fact that the British Royal Family is in different circumstances from all others. Though Scandinavian royalty may move among their people almost as ordinary citizens, that is not possible for the Queen and Prince Philip. Though appeals were made in Sweden for Her Majesty and her husband to be able to have some free time untroubled by crowds, they went unheeded. Everywhere there were cheering crowds. "I have never seen the Swedes behaving like this before—nor have I heard them behaving like this," declared one observer who had lived in Sweden for many years.

While in Sweden the Queen, Prince Philip, and Princess Margaret attended the Olympic Games equestrian events and saw the British team, under Colonel Frank Weldon, carry off the gold medal for the Three-day Event and the show-jumping team gain the bronze medal.

The Royal Family were in residence at Windsor from June 18 until June 23. In the afternoon of June 18 a service of the Order of the Garter was held in St George's Chapel. On the last day of her stay Her Majesty inspected the three hundredth anniversary parade of the Grenadier Guards. On June 26 in Hyde Park the Queen reviewed 300 holders of the Victoria Cross. "To all of us the Victoria Cross is a symbol of the height to which we all can rise at our country's need. But on this proud occasion let us not

The Queen's interest in the welfare of the officers and men of the armed services takes her on many visits to depots and stations. In this picture Her Majesty is seen chatting with a Royal Air Force sergeant and his wife outside their quarters at the R.A.F. Fighter Command Station at Leuchars, Fife, on June 4, 1957.

(By courtesy of the Air Ministry)

Head of ten member nations of the United Nations and greeted by the representatives of all of them, the Queen had a wonderful reception from the General Assembly in New York in October 1957. Here Her Majesty is seen addressing the delegates.

The family at home in London. The Queen and Prince Philip seen at the bridge by the lake in the gardens of Buckingham Palace.

(*Photo Tony Armstrong-Jones*)

forget that courage in battle is only one side of war's account. Do not let us think that it cancels out the suffering and misery which man, whether willingly or unwillingly, has inflicted on man. We must all pray and strive to secure that the account may now be closed," said the Queen.

Mr and Mrs Harry S. Truman lunched at the Palace on June 26, a day on which Mr Robert Menzies, Prime Minister of Australia, and Viscount Malvern, Prime Minister of the Federation of Rhodesia and Nyasaland, came to see Her Majesty. The next day the Queen entertained the Commonwealth Prime Ministers to dinner at the Palace. That day also brought audiences for Mr Holland, the New Zealand Prime Minister, Mr Nehru of India, Mr Strijdom, Prime Minister of South Africa, and on June 28 Mr John Bowlen, Lieutenant-Governor of Alberta.

After a visit to Scotland between July 3 and July 8 the Queen, with Prince Philip, returned to London, and the Prince opened at Oxford his conference on the Human Problems of Industrial Communities. On July 16 King Feisal II of Iraq came to London for a four-day State visit. On July 27 Her Majesty had lunch on board the King of Denmark's yacht in the Thames.

Egypt had seized the Suez Canal on July 26, and while the Queen was at Goodwood Races on August 2 she was shown, in her private room in the Duke of Richmond's box, the text of a Proclamation calling out the Army Reserve. After Her Majesty had approved it the Proclamation was read in the House of Commons. But it was not until the following day, at a special Privy Council at Arundel Castle, where she was staying as the guest of the Duke of Norfolk, that the Queen signed the document.

On August 11 Her Majesty, accompanied by Prince Philip, visited Barrow-in-Furness, and there boarded *Britannia* for a tour of the Western Isles of Scotland.

On August 19 the royal couple attended the opening ceremony of the tenth Edinburgh Festival. Earlier the Queen had for the first time held a Privy Council in the royal yacht *Britannia.* At this Council Her Majesty gave formal assent to the marriage of Captain Alexander Ramsay, son of her cousin, Lady Patricia Ramsay.

While she was at Balmoral in September she received Mr Robert Menzies, the Australian Prime Minister, and Dame Patty Menzies. "I called in to give Her Majesty a little background of my talks with Colonel Nasser in Egypt regarding the future of the Suez Canal," said Mr Menzies.

Prince Philip left London Airport on October 15 for Mombasa on the first stage of his round-the-world journey which would take him to the Olympic Games in Melbourne and afterwards to the Antarctic bases. At 10 P.M. the Queen left for Lanarkshire and Dumfries, but went south to Cumberland on October 17 to open the world's first nuclear-powered generating station at Calder Hall.

Throughout October Her Majesty carried out a wide variety of engagements. On October 19 she entertained the President of Costa Rica and Mme Figueres to lunch at the Palace. On October 25 the Queen attended the performance of *Giselle* by the Bolshoi Ballet Company at the Royal Opera House, Covent Garden. On October 26 the Queen received General Alfred Gruenther, Supreme Allied Commander Europe, and Mrs Gruenther.

A deputation from the Virginia 350th Anniversary Commission, including Mr T. B. Stanley, Governor of Virginia, Mr Lewis McMurman, Chairman of the Commission, and Mrs Parks Rouse junior, director of the

Jamestown Festival, was received by the Queen at Buckingham Palace on October 26. The deputation, apart from giving the Queen an outline of the scope of the celebrations, expressed the hope that the Queen might find it possible to visit the Festival during its course.

Mr Einar Gerhardsen, Prime Minister of Norway, and Mrs Gerhardsen were received at the Palace on October 31. On November 6 Her Majesty opened Parliament, on November 7 held another of her regular luncheon parties, and on November 8 held an evening Presentation Party for members of the Diplomatic Corps, at which Princess Margaret was present. On November 15 the Queen, accompanied by the Queen Mother, was present at an installation service of the Order of the Bath at Westminster Abbey.

When she attended a dinner at the Royal Hospital, Chelsea, on November 27 to celebrate the three hundredth anniversary of the founding of the Standing Army, the Queen, who was the guest of the Army Council, quoted a letter from a soldier to his former colonel. Colour Sergeant William Wykes wrote: "You will see by the address that disaster has overtaken me. I feel something like a man who has awakened from an operation to find himself minus a limb. They have taken away my cap badge and with it the great love of my life. The traditions of my county regiment (the Sherwood Foresters) are in my blood, and to be known as a Forester was an estate of which I was deeply proud."

"That is how one British soldier feels about his regiment," said the Queen. "The British Army has always been small. It has always been a family affair—a family centring on the regiment, and it has lived by quality more than by its size."

During the year work had been proceeding on the State apartments of Kensington Palace. The King's Gallery had been redecorated with a brocaded paper in blue and gold; the King's Drawing Room had been papered in green; and the fireplaces which had been filled in after Queen Victoria left the Palace in 1837 were cleared again.

On November 28 the Queen visited Kensington Palace to see the rooms which had been furnished with a great many pieces from the collection of Queen Mary. Her Majesty also inspected the bedroom from which Queen Victoria was called to her accession. This room had been restored to almost exactly as it was on the early morning of June 20, 1837. The young Queen's heavy satinwood bed with its green-flowered bedspread and the washstand in the corner were all on view. So too was the last dress worn by Queen Victoria, a black, dull silk dress, heavily bordered with mourning crêpe.

Princess Marie Louise, granddaughter of Queen Victoria and "Cousin Louie" to the Queen, died on December 8. Her Majesty had lost one of her closest friends, whose reminiscences of bygone days never failed to charm and whose wise counsels had often been appreciated. Princess Marie Louise was a democrat who had loved to mix with the ordinary people, and shortly before her death she recorded many of these meetings in a book entitled *My Memories of Six Reigns*, which, she herself revealed, the Queen had suggested she should write. The Princess said that one day Her Majesty, listening to some charming story of long ago, said, "Cousin Louie, you must write it all down as a book." Princess Marie Louise did so, every word written with a very soft pencil in her own neat longhand.

The funeral took place at St George's Chapel, Windsor

Castle, on December 14, and the Princess whom Queen Victoria had once described in a letter as "poor little Louise very ugly" was buried in the royal vault.

During 1956 the Queen, in addition to her visits to Nigeria and Sweden, carried out 402 public engagements.

15

"Don't Go Home"

THERE can never be a complete holiday for the Sovereign, however much the Governments of the Commonwealth keep down the enormous number of documents which every day come on to the Queen's desk. By January 1, 1957, the Queen realized that she was facing the most crowded year of her life, with visits to Portugal, France, and Denmark already planned and the possibility (soon confirmed) of one to the United States and Canada. The Suez crisis threw an enormous amount of work on Her Majesty, and her Sandringham holiday was constantly interrupted by the Middle East troubles and their political repercussions.

On January 8 Sir Anthony and Lady Eden travelled to Sandringham, and it was thought that this was merely the usual audience for the Prime Minister. In fact, at that meeting Sir Anthony told Her Majesty that because of his doctor's report on his health he could not continue in office. It was arranged that the Queen should travel up to London on the following day for further consultations and for the formal announcement of the Prime Minister's resignation.

There was at first no suspicion in the public mind that the Queen's return to London was anything more than a shopping trip. Even the calling of a Cabinet meeting did not give rise to a resignation rumour until the afternoon. But when at eight minutes past six in the evening Sir Anthony left 10 Downing Street and drove towards the Palace the news that he was to resign spread. At seven o'clock the announcement was issued from the Palace.

There was a short period of intense speculation throughout the country as to who would be called upon to lead the Government. The Conservative Party had no elected party leader, although Mr R. A. Butler was generally supposed to be next in line of succession to Sir Anthony. Still, there were many who favoured Mr Harold Macmillan. This doubt and difference reacted in an unfortunate and unexpected way.

In the morning of January 10 the Queen saw Lord Salisbury, Lord President of the Council, and soon afterwards Sir Winston Churchill drove up to the Palace and saw Her Majesty. When Mr Harold Macmillan drove into the forecourt just before 2 P.M. the waiting crowd knew that the succession had passed to him and not to Mr Butler.

To the surprise of many ordinary citizens, a political storm blew up immediately. The Parliamentary Labour Party talked of the constitutional implications of the way in which Mr Macmillan had been selected to succeed Sir Anthony Eden. The Labour leaders felt that the Queen had been forced to make a choice between two potential leaders of the Conservative Party, and thereby had herself decided that leadership in advance. While they made no reflection on the propriety of the Queen's exercise of her constitutional duty on advice tendered to her in a difficult situation, the Labour leaders thought that she was confronted by a position that could well have involved her in party politics.

Not only was Her Majesty involved, however remotely,

in a party political squabble, but her action in travelling to London on the following Sunday to receive the Prime Minister brought a rebuke for Mr Macmillan (a regular churchgoer himself) from the members of the Lord's Day Observance Society, which, by inference, was directed also to the Queen. "We are grieved that you sought an audience with Her Majesty the Queen on Sunday last in order to submit to her the names of the members of the new Cabinet. We note that this necessitated Her Majesty travelling from Sandringham on Sunday. To some this may seem but a small thing, but in our opinion it is unfortunately typical of the national disregard for the sanctity of God's Holy Day," the letter ran. In April the Society rebuked Mr Peter Thorneycroft for presenting his Budget proposals to the Queen on a Sunday.

Here was one more example of a departure from the old dictum "The King can do no wrong." In matters of everyday concern it is often true that the "Queen can do no right" in the eyes of some vociferous minorities. No single year passes without an attack being made on Her Majesty's appearance on Sunday afternoons at some sporting occasion (usually polo at Windsor or Cowdray). This year, apart from the rebukes of the Lord's Day Observance Society already mentioned, there was to follow, in March, a sharp attack from members of the League Against Cruel Sports. One member went so far as to say, "We know who our chief enemies are—and the Queen is certainly our worst enemy."

Criticism of the sovereign is nothing new in Britain. Indeed, Queen Elizabeth II suffers less from adverse criticism and attack than did Queen Victoria. It is a measure of the place that the Queen occupies in the hearts of the people that her everyday actions, constantly in the limelight as they are, so rarely offend even the most susceptible and sensitive people. But unfair criticism—and most that is directed against the Queen is unfair, as witness the protest that she actually went horse-racing on the day that Parliament reassembled to debate Suez—is ill-considered and stupid and does not make a hard and difficult job any easier.

At a time when she would normally just be settling down to the official engagements in London the Queen set out for the first of the overseas visits during 1957—her four-day visit to Portugal. This was a return visit for the trip to London of General Craveiro Lopes and Senhora Lopes in October 1955, but in addition it was the occasion for the reunion of the Queen with Prince Philip after his round-the-world voyage.

The reception of the Queen in Lisbon was tremendous. As the royal yacht *Britannia* dropped anchor in the Tagus the hooting of sirens of hundreds of craft of all sizes mingled with the roars of cheering from tens of thousands of people. The Portuguese royal barge brought the Queen ashore, a barge that had been used only once since it brought King Edward VII ashore from the royal yacht *Victoria and Albert* in 1903. Eighty bargemen in red shirts manned this gilded craft which brought the Queen and Prince Philip to the wharf where the Portuguese President and his wife waited.

But the public celebration of the traditional friendship between Britain and Portugal could not please every one. Her Majesty was subject to an attack in the *Economic Review*, issued by the All-India Congress Committee, which in an article criticized her visit to Portugal. Mr Nehru, the Indian Prime Minister, was swift to express his regrets at the article. "I deeply regret the publication of this note, which is wholly intemperate and in very bad taste," he said. "I am particularly disturbed that the Queen's name should be brought into this, and I should like to offer my apologies to her."

The Portuguese visit ended in one of those happy and spontaneous gestures for which the royal travellers are becoming famous. After their last official function the Queen and Prince Philip travelled to the airport on the back seat of a police bus. Her Majesty and the Prince realized that the closed car in which they had been travelling made it impossible for the people who filled all the windows along the route, and even many in the roadside crowds, to see them. In the bus they were not only visible, but in the open, and the people showed their appreciation by throwing roses and camellias into the bus until it was almost filled with flowers. As the royal plane took off the crowds burst through the barriers and lined the runway, so that they were no more than a few yards from the wing-tips as the aircraft sped past to become airborne.

Back in London on February 21, the Queen held, on February 27, another of the new-style luncheon parties at Buckingham Palace which had begun on May 11 the year before. On the Queen's right sat the Right Rev. Cyril Eastaugh, Bishop of Kensington; on her left Sir Norman Brook, joint Permanent Secretary to the Treasury. On Prince Philip's right was Flora Robson, the actress; on his left Sir Vincent Tewson, General Secretary of the Trades Union Congress. Sir Henry Spurrier, Managing Director of Leyland Motors, Ltd, Sir Norman Kipping, Director-General of the Federation of British Industries, and Mr J. Arthur Rank were also present. The conversation ranged over a wide field of subjects. Miss Flora Robson revealed afterwards that beards, hypnotism, blind people (the Queen remarked how she was always touched by the way blind people could laugh at their mistakes), had been among the topics discussed. For Her Majesty it was another excellent opportunity of feeling the pulse of the nation by contact with ordinary men and women in all walks of life in the community.

On March 1 the Queen, accompanied by Prince Philip, went to Harwell to see the Radiochemistry Department and to start the new Dido reactor on full power. At the reactor school they talked to students from Canada, Australia, India, Pakistan, South Africa, and New Zealand.

The Queen was without her personal maid during the first part of March. Miss Margaret MacDonald, whom the Queen calls "Bobo," the fifty-two-year-old maid who has been with Her Majesty for more than twenty years, having charge of her wardrobe on almost all the overseas tours, was taken ill and sent to hospital. On March 9 the Queen drove to the London Hospital to see Miss MacDonald, who was in a private ward, to take her flowers and sit with her for more than half an hour. Sir Horace Evans, the Queen's physician, was attending Miss MacDonald. Reasons why the London Hospital was chosen, although it is some miles from Buckingham Palace, and other hospitals are closer, are that the Queen is Patron and Sir Horace is on the medical staff.

On April 8 the Queen with Prince Philip flew to Paris for her State visit, a visit that was to revive all the glories of the Entente Cordiale. "Our emotion will be shared by all my people, for it is my people that you are greeting through us," the Queen said at the end of a day in which Parisians had produced an exhibition of affection and happiness that can hardly have been matched in any capital. "My people fully reciprocate all the sympathy and affection that you are showing for us," said Her Majesty.

Both M. Coty, the French President, and the Queen referred to the Entente Cordiale in their speeches at the State Banquet at the Élysée Palace. M. Coty reminded his hearers of the work of King Edward VII for friendship between the two countries. He also quoted the lines by Ronsard which were dedicated to Queen Elizabeth I.

> Quand vous serez ensemble bien unies
> L'amour, la foi, deux belles compagnies,
> Viennent cy-bas le cœur vous rechauffer.

> ("When together you are completely united
> Love and faith, those beautiful companions,
> Descend to warm your hearts.")

"The example of the two countries in overlooking the differences and antagonisms of several centuries has acquired a meaning without precedent during the past half-century, particularly since ten years of the most formidable trials in our history have transformed the young Entente into an indissoluble unity for ever sealed by the blood that so many sons of the United Kingdom and of the Republic shed side by side," declared the President.

At the Opera, when Her Majesty appeared on the balcony, an estimated half a million people, massed as far down as the Louvre, gave an immense and spontaneous cry of pleasure and admiration that was as much a tribute of friendship as it was to beauty and grace.

The grandeur of the river pageants as the Queen and Prince Philip were taken along the Seine in a launch, the visit to Versailles and to the industrial North—all of these events brought new meaning and new strength to the grand alliance.

The Queen and Prince Philip came back with unforgettable memories of a wonderful visit—of the immense crowd before the Opera, of the glories of Versailles, of the incident when President Coty, having decorated Prince Philip with the Legion of Honour, turned to the Queen, bowed, and said, "Et maintenant, Madame, l'accolade," inviting Her Majesty to kiss her husband. There were the wonderful occasions when French Communist workers outdid the cheering of their fellows and waved a forest of Union Jacks, of others who support the Communist Party who had placed a Union Jack on their concrete-mixer; of the overwhelming reception in the industrial towns of Northern France; of the great firework display which brought the river pageant to an end. Finally there was the incident of their leaving, when, opposite the Gare du Nord, a man stood with a huge poster which bore the words "Don't Go Home," a sentiment that all France was sharing at that moment.

On April 18 Her Majesty distributed the Royal Maundy at St Albans Cathedral. On April 28 the Queen took the salute from 1000 Queen's Scouts at Windsor Castle. On May 4 she visited the Royal Naval College, Greenwich, to meet the senior naval officers of the Commonwealth attending a course. Her Majesty saw in one of the halls much of the new equipment both for attack and for defence now being adopted by the Commonwealth navies.

The visit to Denmark began on May 21 after the Queen and Prince Philip had toured Hull on May 18. This was a royal visit abroad such as rarely takes place—days of good humour and easygoing activity. The visit began on a note of laughter—if lumbago can ever be laughable—for the King of Denmark had difficulty in moving on account of a sudden and sharp attack. That laughter went on throughout the visit, so that the Queen and Prince Philip were able to make a holiday out of their stay in a way that is rarely possible. It was a rest-cure that was welcome, for the Queen had carried out almost 200 engagements since the opening of the year.

Everywhere there was laughter, everywhere an obvious inexperience of the way in which great royal occasions are usually arranged. The guests at functions stood up when they should have remained seated or remained seated when they should have stood up, cheered when cheering was not in order, and remained silent when a cheer was called for. But every one remained good-humoured about it all, and the Queen was so obviously enjoying every minute of her stay that no one was distressed. And Her Majesty could be forgiven for wishing that the easy formality of the Danish king's life could sometimes be hers. Yet, because the crowds were so unusually demonstrative whenever she appeared, a planned visit to the famous Tivoli Gardens in Copenhagen had to be cancelled.

The royal yacht *Britannia* carried the Queen and Prince Philip to a review of the Home Fleet at Invergordon on May 27. And so into June—the Trooping the Colour ceremony on Horse Guards; a Buckingham Palace welcome to delegates to the Nigeria conference on self-determination, swift and practical putting into effect of the Queen's lesson in unity of only twelve months before; a Garter service at Windsor. Royal Ascot came again, with the Queen's horses winning new triumphs in a triumphant season. This had started for Her Majesty on May 18, when, for the first time, the Queen had a racing treble. Three horses bred at the royal stud—Pall Mall, Atlas, and Might and Main—all won at Haydock Park. At Epsom, although her Doutelle had disappointed in the Derby, her filly Carozza won the Oaks, and at Royal Ascot her filly Almeria won the Ribblesdale Stakes.

On June 11 there was another in the series of informal lunches at the Palace. Among the guests of the Queen and Prince Philip was Mr Justice Devlin, who had judged the trial of Dr Bodkin Adams. Also round the table were Sir Ernest Oppenheimer, the South African diamond millionaire, and Lady Oppenheimer; Mr Kenneth Younger, Labour M.P. for Grimsby; the Right Rev. Joost de Blank, Archbishop of Cape Town; Major Sir William Anstruther-Gray, Conservative M.P. for Berwick and East Lothian; Mr Charles Wheeler, President of the Royal Academy; and Mr Isaiah Berlin, Fellow of All Souls, Oxford, philosopher and historian. The talk ranged over a great variety of subjects—famous law cases, South Africa and the United States, where Mr Berlin once lectured in universities and also served in the Washington Embassy.

The Commonwealth Prime Ministers dined in ancient St George's Hall, Windsor Castle, on June 26, and the Windsor gold plate graced the long table that had the Queen at its head. On July 1 Her Majesty attended the hundred-and-fiftieth-anniversary celebrations at Mill Hill School.

When the Queen welcomed the 4000 members of the American Bar Association at a garden party at Buckingham Palace on July 29 she served 'hot dogs' as part of the refreshments. Her Majesty regarded this visit as of the greatest importance in the pattern of Anglo-American relations.

While she was at Balmoral on August 23 the Queen held a Privy Council at which the final constitutional decisions leading to the independence of Malaya were considered and agreed.

16

The Weapon of Example

It was perhaps significant that a year which brought to the Queen her busiest twelve months and some of her greatest triumphs should also witness the greatest number of and most outspoken attacks on herself and her Court. Following the early criticisms of the Lord's Day Observance Society and the League Against Cruel Sports came comments from Lord Altrincham in his monthly political magazine; from Mr B. A. Young, a journalist; by Mr John Osborne, a playwright; once more by the Lord's Day Observance Society; and by Mr Malcolm Muggeridge, former editor of *Punch*.

Among Lord Altrincham's strictures, which received world-wide publicity, was the comment that "the personality conveyed by the utterances which are put into her mouth is that of a priggish schoolgirl." Mr Young said, "The Royal Family have plenty of time on their hands; 30-odd public appearances in 90 days is hardly a back-breaking programme for a company whose principal *raison d'être* is the making of public appearances." Mr John Osborne declared in an article that "Nobody can seriously pretend that the royal round of gracious boredom, the protocol of ancient fatuity, is politically useful or morally stimulating." Mr Muggeridge expressed the opinion that "Duchesses find the Queen dowdy, frumpish, and banal."

As usual, there was no shortage of Queen's champions. They pointed out that she had no chance of defending herself, but it was left to Her Majesty to demonstrate that verbal defence could not possibly be so devastating as the powerful weapons of public example and action.

On September 12 the Queen opened the annual conference of the Inter-Parliamentary Union in Westminster Hall, and, though her speech was no different from many she had made before, and though she, in fact, read considerable passages of it, her demeanour—assured and completely at ease—was such as to make foolish the criticisms that she always "read her speeches." Nor could her reminder that political life in all the nations of the Commonwealth of which she was the head was based on parliamentary government be described as the views of "a priggish schoolgirl."

Nor, indeed, could the programme carried out by the Queen in Canada and America be described, even by her most violent critics, as "hardly a backbreaking programme," with its dozen and more engagements a day. The attention that Her Majesty's dresses received from millions of people in North America, and the immediate response in the form of a rush of orders from that continent for British-made clothes, also suggested that if duchesses found the Queen "dowdy" and "frumpish" the fashion-conscious women of the United States and Canada admired her taste in dress. And the world-wide acclamation of the diplomatic triumphs of Her Majesty gave the lie to any assertion that "Nobody can pretend that the royal round is politically useful."

The royal tour of North America was acclaimed as a triumph from beginning to end. The Queen's visit to Canada—which public-opinion polls had suggested left

Canadians lukewarm in their interest—resulted in hundreds of thousands of people flocking into Ottawa from all parts of the vast country. Canadians welcomed their own Queen, and out of that welcome will come most surely a much more close association between Canada and the Crown. Already the idea of a permanent royal residence in Canada has been discussed, and the project is now being studied in the light of prime costs and upkeep and the inevitable reaction from other parts of the Commonwealth.

Her Majesty's television broadcast, the first time she had ever taken part in a solo broadcast on television, was carried through with such assurance as to make laughable accusations that she possesses a style of speaking which is "a pain in the neck" and that she is incapable of stringing "even a few sentences together without a written text." Here was a sincere performance for all to see and understand. And in that speech the Queen revealed that she was already planning more frequent visits in the future.

Mr John Diefenbaker, the Prime Minister, had a surprise audience of the Queen on October 13, at which he revealed the wish of the Canadian Government that Prince Philip might be made a Canadian Privy Councillor. Prince Philip joins the only three other non-Canadians who have been made members of the Council—the Duke of Windsor, Sir Winston Churchill, and Earl Alexander, former Governor-General.

When she wore her Coronation gown at the opening of the Canadian Parliament on October 14 the Queen had worn it publicly to open four Commonwealth Parliaments—Australian, New Zealand, Ceylonese, and Canadian—a record number of appearances for any Coronation gown in British history. Her Majesty recalled the words of Elizabeth I, " 'Though God hath raised me high, yet this I count the glory of my crown—that I have reigned with your loves.'

"Now, here in the New World, I say to you that it is my wish that in the years before me I may so reign in Canada and be so remembered," she declared.

Greatest triumph of the Canadian visit was the Queen's decision that when she flew into the United States she would go as Queen of Canada. With that one announcement Her Majesty confirmed the status of Canada as that of a front-rank Power and revealed to the people of North America that Canada is the natural bridge between the New and the Old Worlds.

At the Government reception at the Château Laurier Hotel on October 15 the Queen and Prince Philip shook hands for 90 minutes non-stop with 1300 guests, and there were many comments on the "phenomenal memory" of the Duke. Prince Philip recognized many people he had met only casually on his last visit to Canada, and recalled minute details of the meeting.

After the reception there was a small—20 strong—dinner party at the Prime Minister's house at 24 Sussex Drive.

There were some who questioned the wisdom of the Queen's visit to Williamsburg and Jamestown before her call at Washington. They had forgotten the visit of the organizers of the Virginia three-hundred-and-fiftieth anniversary Commission to Buckingham Palace in October 1956, when the first steps towards the North American visit were taken. After that visit there had followed many consultations with President Eisenhower. The visit to Williamsburg was regarded by the President, as well as by the Queen, as the ideal means by which the identity of origins as well as of interest of the British and American peoples could be proclaimed to the world.

The great moment of the tour came in the tumultuous welcome of Washington to Her Majesty and Prince Philip. Washington has many reminders of the old days of colonialism and, unlike Williamsburg and Virginia in general, has ideas of resenting them. The Queen's speech at Williamsburg, when she said how she was charmed to hear that Virginia had counties named after every British sovereign from Elizabeth I to George III—she paused and added, "even George III"—was heard and read by millions of Americans who welcomed its candour. And Washington gave the royal visitors a reception such as no foreign visit has ever been accorded in living memory.

Visits to football games and supermarkets might be construed as seeking popularity. The Queen and Prince Philip showed that in fact they were undertaken in order that they might meet the ordinary people. "If this can happen in America why not in Britain?" asked the accompanying journalists, forgetting the informal polo meetings at Windsor and Cowdray Park, the cricket on the village greens and horse shows at Badminton and Windsor when the Queen and her husband sit with the rest of the people and for a while completely lose their identity in the crowd.

New York has known more tons of ticker tape, but never a bigger crowd nor greater enthusiasm, and the feelings of the vast crowds along Broadway were summed up by an Irish-American policeman who said, "I think she's real fine, and anyone who can go through what she is going through is O.K. in my book."

No visitor to the United States, in fact, has ever had so time- and energy-consuming a schedule of events. In

President Eisenhower and Mrs Eisenhower greet the Queen and Prince Philip on the steps of the White House, Washington, during the triumphant royal tour of North America.

" Chicago Tribune," Photo by Al Madsen

Jamestown and Williamsburg the official day included sixteen separate ceremonies, culminating in a great banquet given by Governor Stanley of Virginia. But in that crowded day the Queen had been able to remind all Americans that "the settlement in Jamestown was the beginning of a series of overseas settlements made throughout the world by British pioneers. Jamestown grew and became the United States. Those other countries grew and became nations now united in our great Commonwealth."

This reminder of the common heritage of the two great federations was not lost on Americans at a time when they were engrossed in speculation about the extent to which Russian scientists had gone ahead of their own in the design and manufacture of inter-continental ballistic missiles. The assurance of a common beginning and a common interest to-day was cheering even to a nation which was fully conscious of its power.

A surge of pride went out across the whole of the continent as the pageant of history unfolded on countless television screens. Her Majesty's message brought a new understanding of the past and a new appreciation of the present.

In Washington on the first day there were nine engagements crowded into an afternoon and evening, including a Press conference which gave the Queen and Prince Philip an opportunity of dispelling any doubts the newspapermen may have had about their ability to 'mix.' Next day there were fourteen engagements, and the day following thirteen separate functions, including the memorable football game between the Universities of Maryland and North Carolina at which the royal visitors were greeted by a spirited if unusual version of "Rule, Britannia!" and by a Union Jack formed by a forest of cards.

In all the stay in Washington there was only one private engagement—a visit to the vast Middleburg horse-training centre of Mr and Mrs Paul Mellon, where the Queen revealed her 'eye' for a horse and her knowledge of the American stud-book. Mrs Mellon had had timber cradles erected round the flowerbeds outside her home to carry protective cotton covers to guard the flowers against damage from night cold so that they would make the best possible show for the visit. "The garden looked as if we had hung out the wash," she said.

In the cool, white home of her hosts Her Majesty discussed breeding and training problems and talked over the possibility of more frequent 'challenge' races in which British horses would race against America's best. The Queen recalled the disappointing form of her own Landau in 1954 when it ran last in the Washington International Meeting at Laurel Park, Maryland.

A great crowd bade farewell to the royal visitors when they took train for New York. One commentator described the Queen in unusual terms: "There goes Britain's ultimate diplomatic weapon." But unusual terms were frequent as Americans tried to describe their impressions of Her Majesty. Sixty-seven-year-old President Eisenhower himself, in an aside, was heard to say of his thirty-one-year-old guest: "She is a good girl. She is all right."

At the United Nations in New York the Queen received a standing ovation from the delegates—there seemed to be more than ordinary warmth in the clapping, for here was the head of ten member nations of the Organization—a unique occurrence as it was a unique position. "When justice and respect for obligations are firmly established the United Nations will the more confidently achieve the goal of a world at peace, law-abiding and prosperous, for which men and women have striven so long and which is the heart's desire of every nation here represented," said Her Majesty, whose composure and calm brought murmurs of admiration from all the public galleries.

Later, at the banquet of the Pilgrims and the English-Speaking Union at the Waldorf-Astoria Hotel, the biggest crowd of personalities ever assembled at a New York dinner paid farewell homage—and it was truly homage for a magnificent job—to the Queen and Prince Philip. Five overflow banqueting-rooms had to be called into use, and the guests in these watched and listened to the proceedings on television screens.

The Queen, with the television cameras recording her every movement for millions of viewers throughout the country, declared, "On the maintenance of understanding between us the future of the free world depends."

Last official function of the North American visit was a Commonwealth Ball on fashionable Park Avenue where the Queen and Prince Philip met the presidents of the St Andrew's, St George's, St David's, Ulster Irish, Canadian, and Australian Societies in the United States. At the Ball 4500 people crowded into the huge New York Armoury of the 7th Regiment, and the Queen and Prince Philip were greeted by guards of honour of British ex-Servicemen, the Royal Canadian Navy, and a unit of the 7th Regiment in grey and white ceremonial uniforms.

When the royal couple came out of the ballroom to drive to the airport for the flight back across the Atlantic the crowds were massed on the pavement and the cheering was deafening in its enthusiasm, even the security police joining in. Here was full evidence of the place the royal visitors had won in the minds and hearts of New Yorkers.

In London on October 22 the welcome from a huge

crowd at the airport was more sober, but the citizens who cheered the returned travellers gave evidence that they understood the service that the Queen and Prince Philip had given to the Commonwealth cause. Behind them in the United States they had left a people who had never been closer to the British Commonwealth nor more well disposed. There could be no greater service to the free nations than that.

Ten years had passed since the Queen's dedication to service. In that time she had carried out more than 4000 engagements of all kinds. She has brought a new democracy to the Court. She has reached the hearts and interests of her subjects in all parts of the world as no previous sovereign has ever been able to. She has unified the Commonwealth and has bound together nations of differing colour, race, and interests. She has given to all of them a conception of co-operation that is the marvel and often the envy of the rest of the world. She has remained at the same time a Queen, regal and sometimes imperious, firm and strong-willed, wise in counsel beyond her years and experience because she has taken pains to understand her subjects; Christian in thought and action and passionately devoted to the well-being of the nations who are honoured by having her as their head.

HIGHGATE INSTITUTION

Index

INDEX

INSTITUTION